ONE DIRECTION
Coloring Book

Jack Anthony

ISBN-13:
978-1484086735

ISBN-10:
1484086732

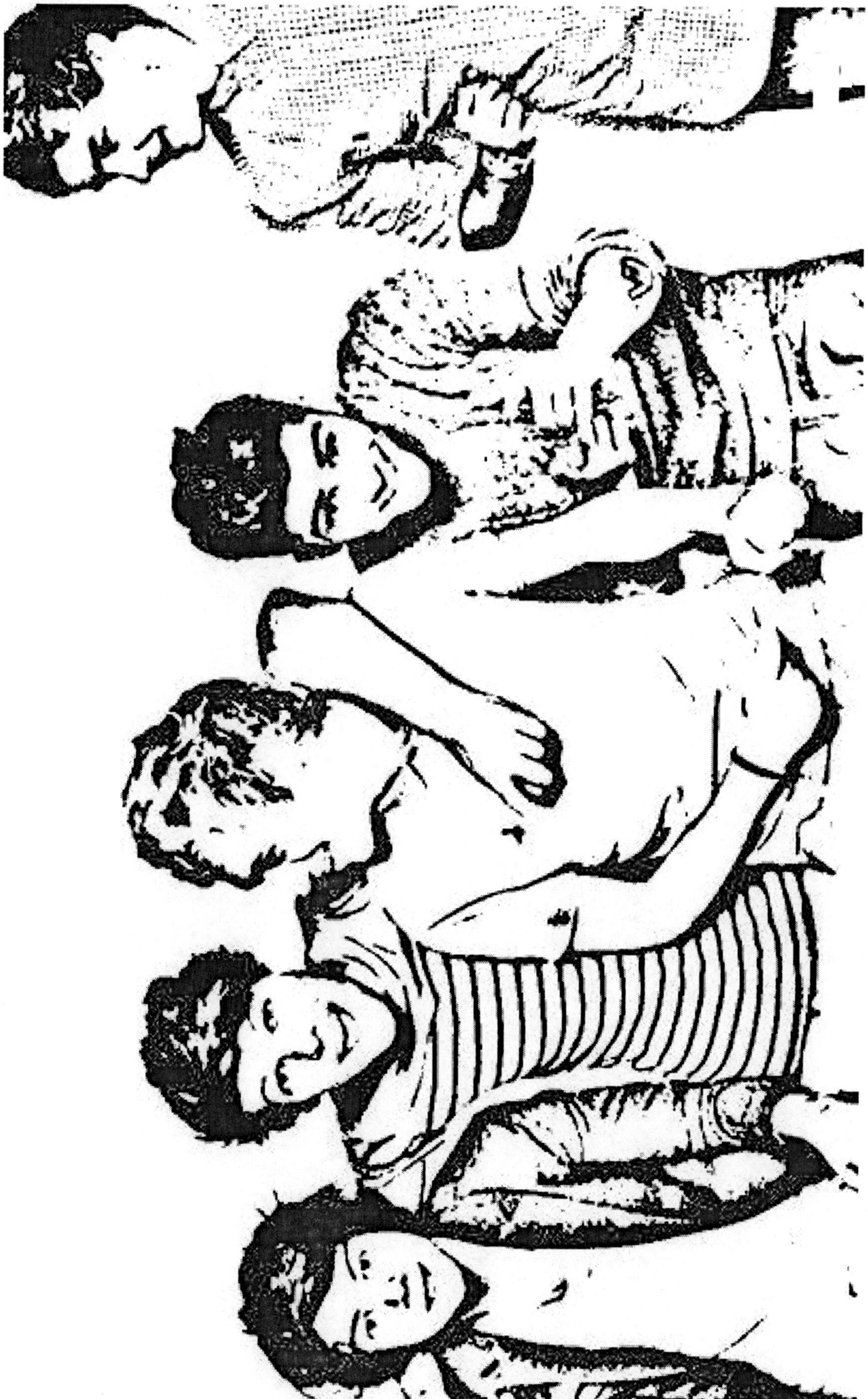

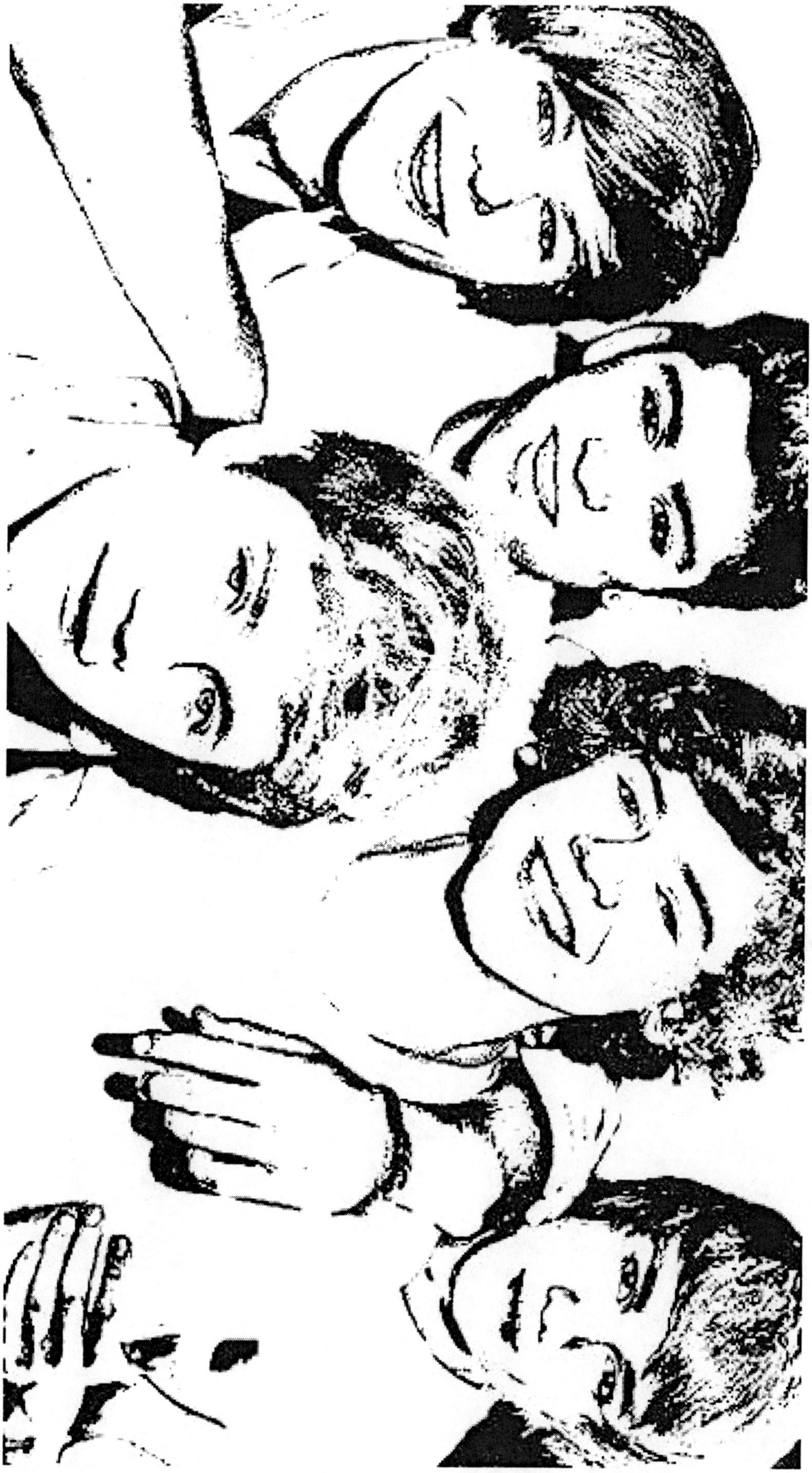

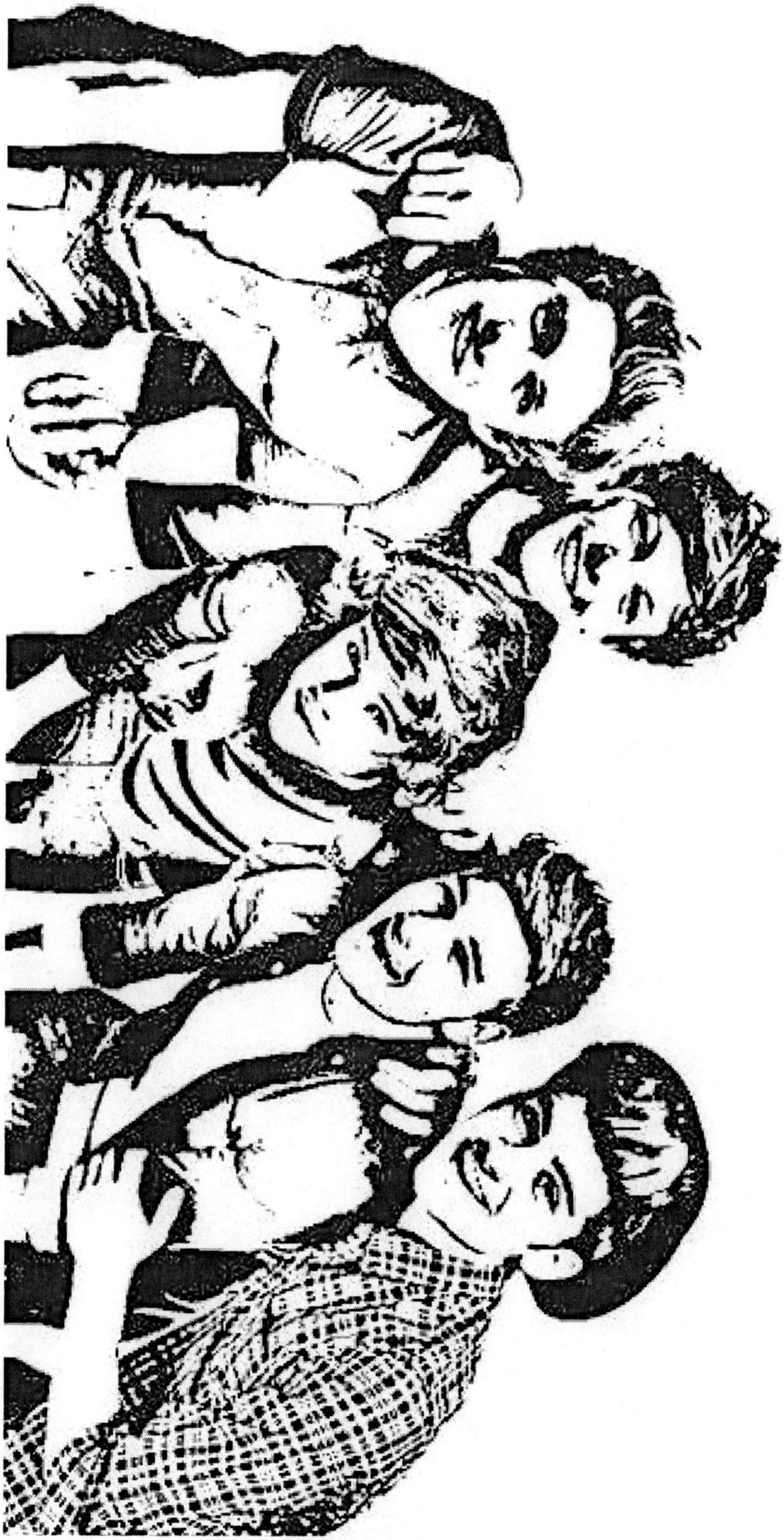

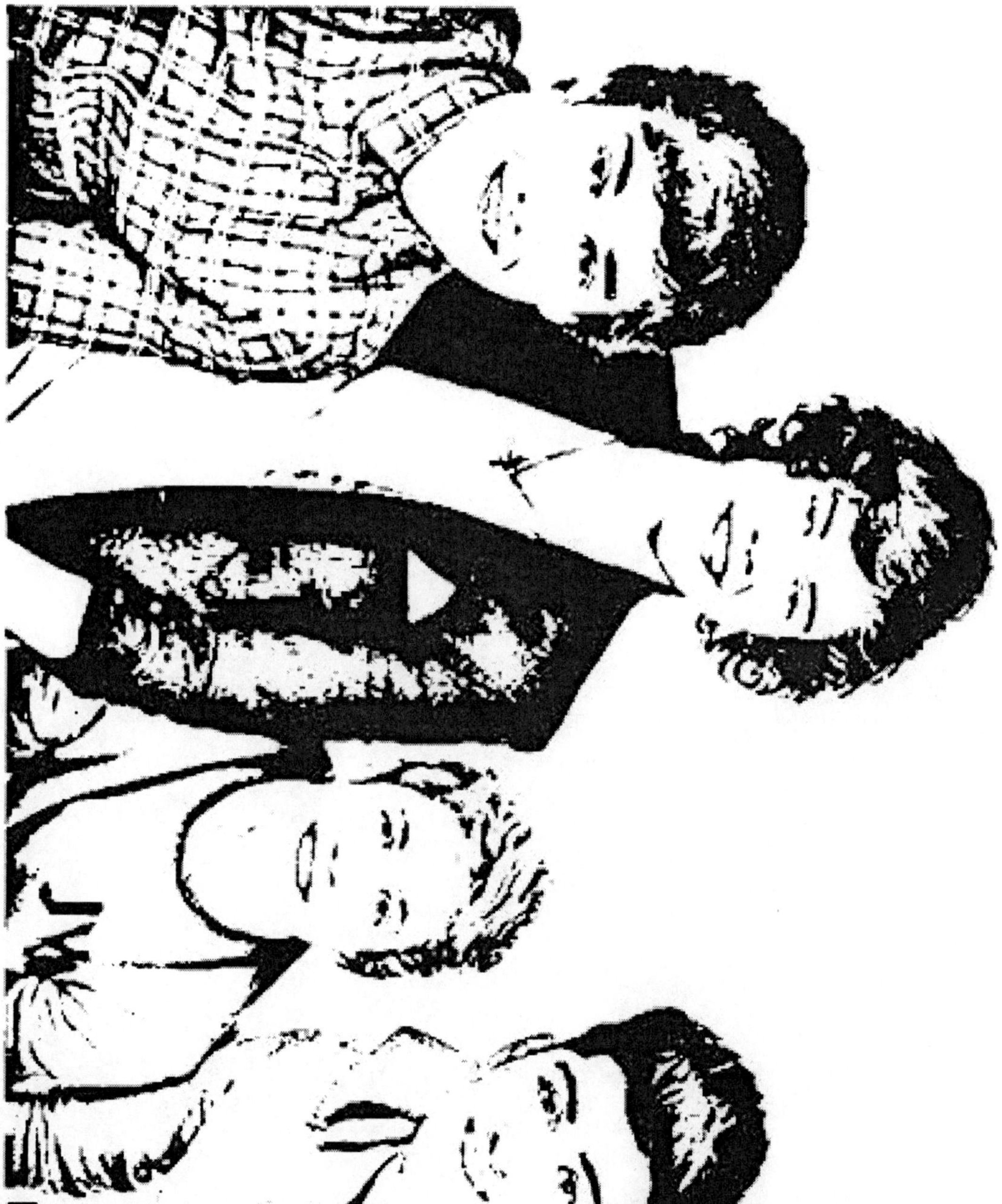

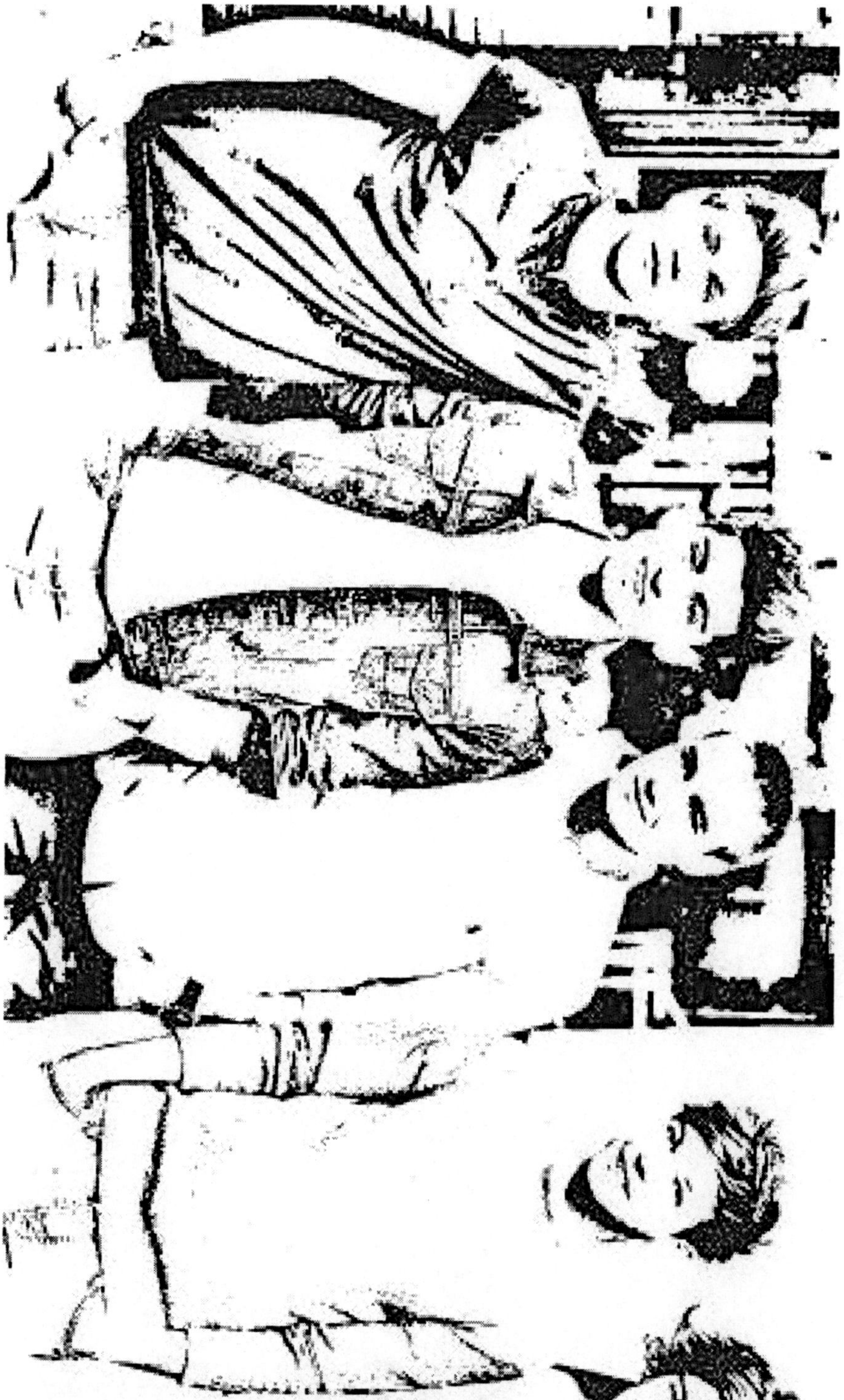

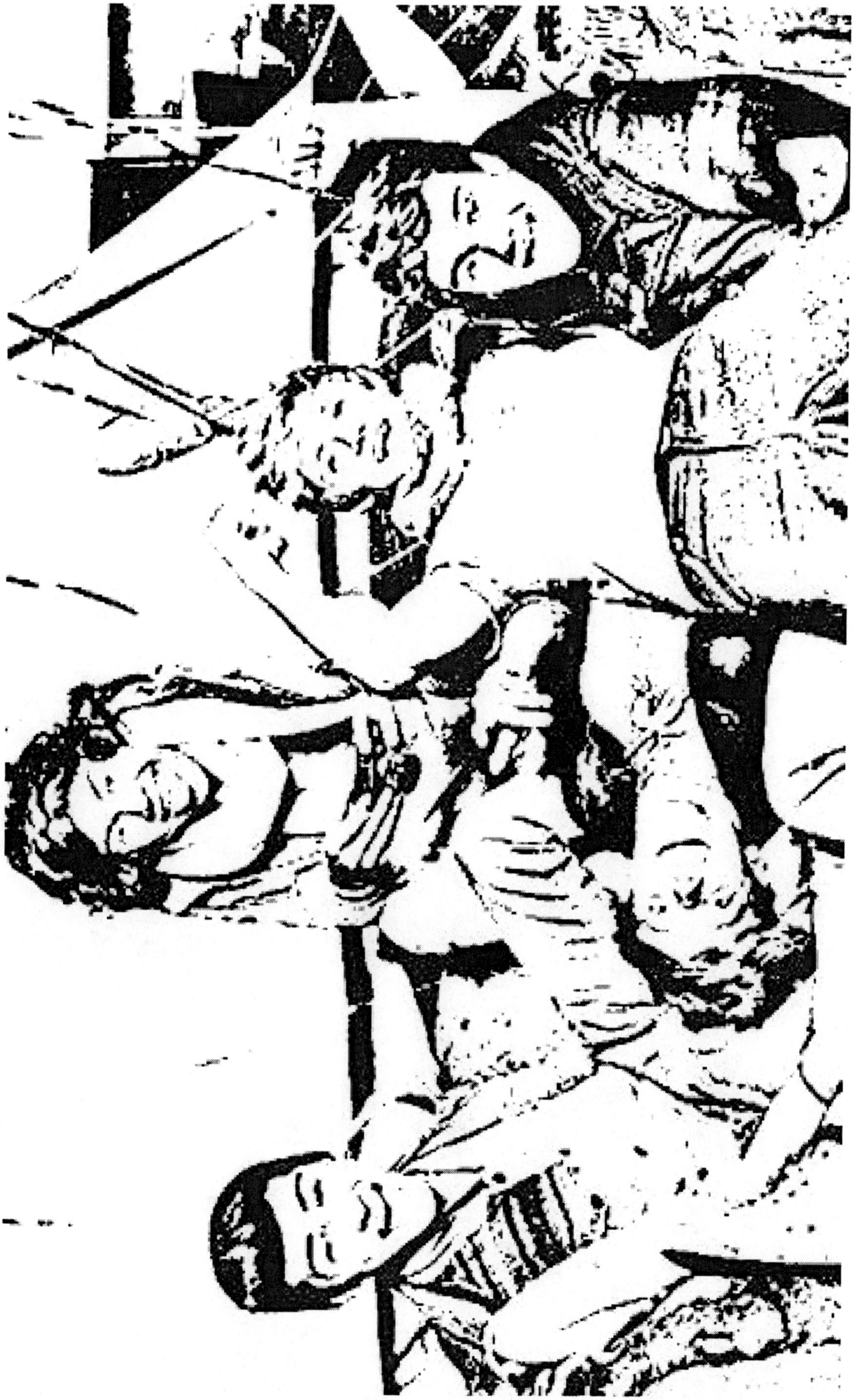

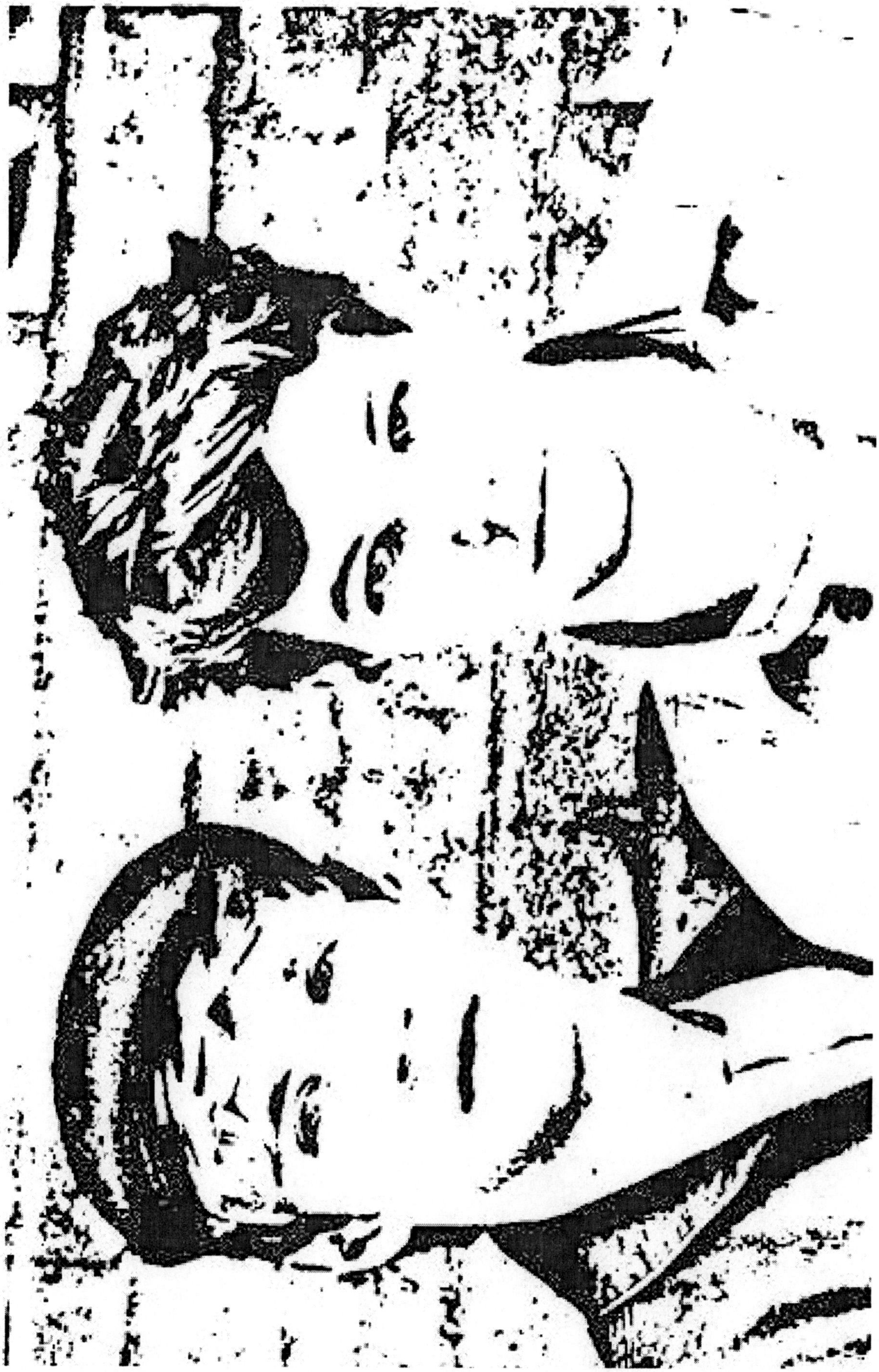

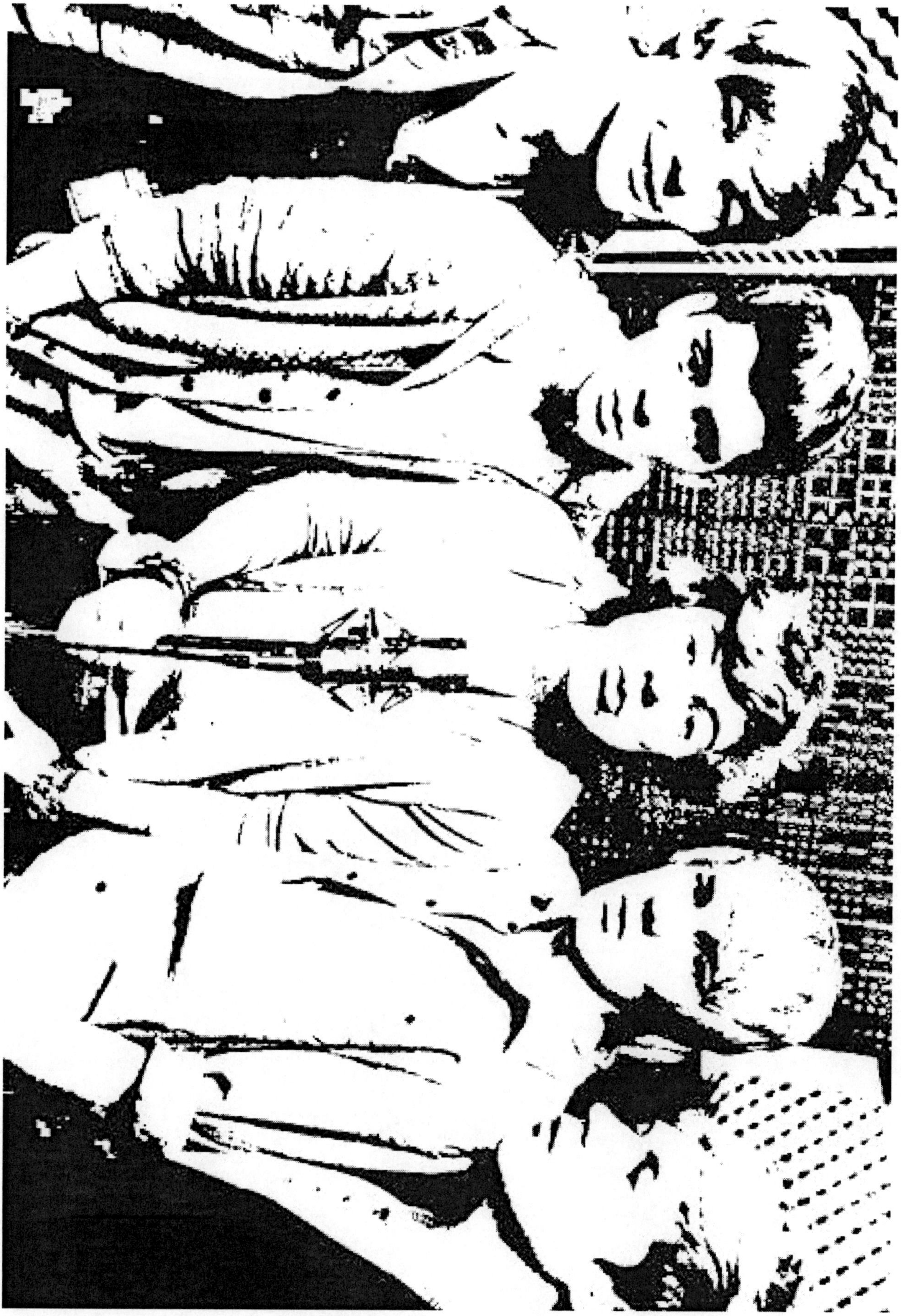

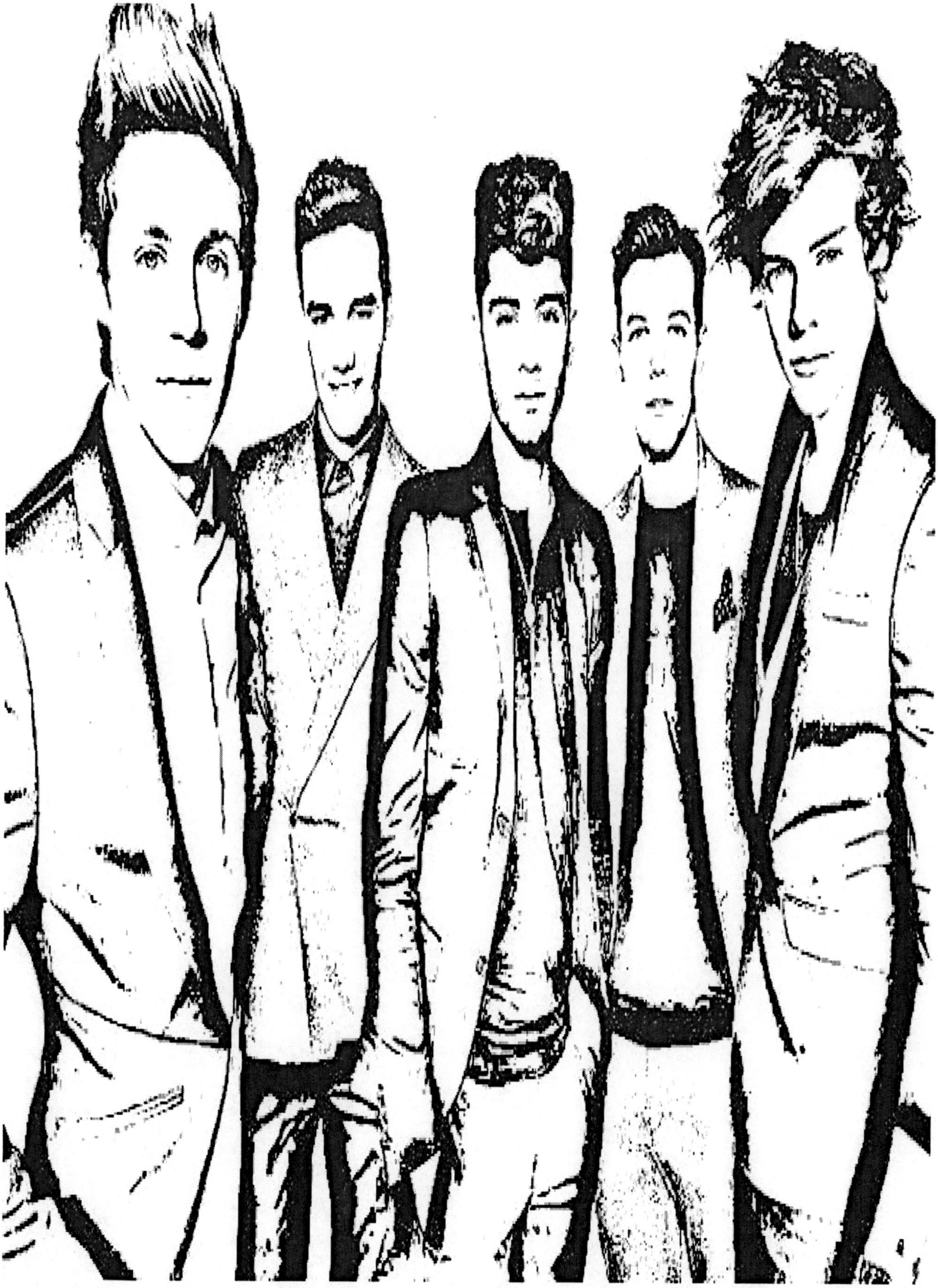

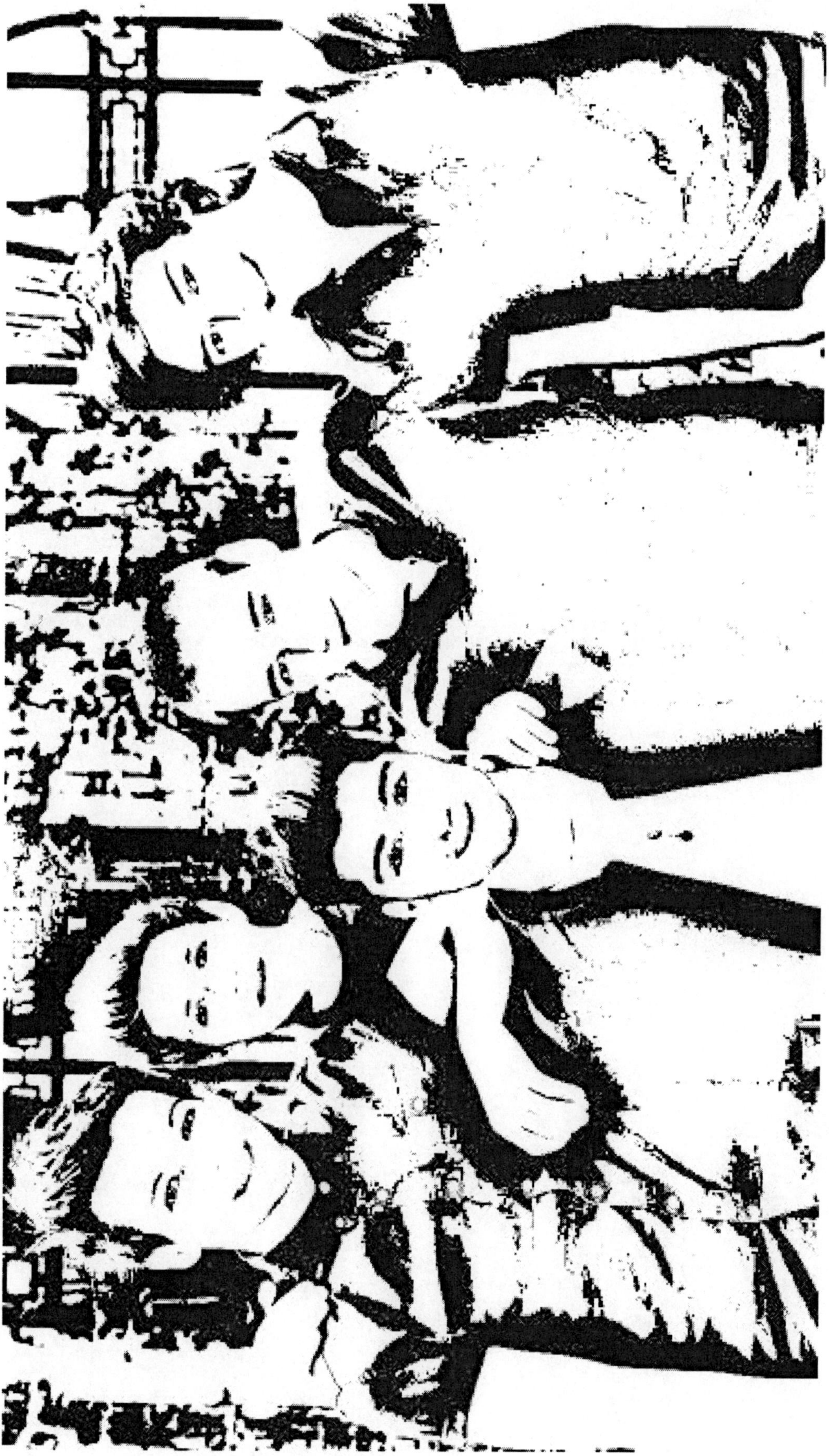

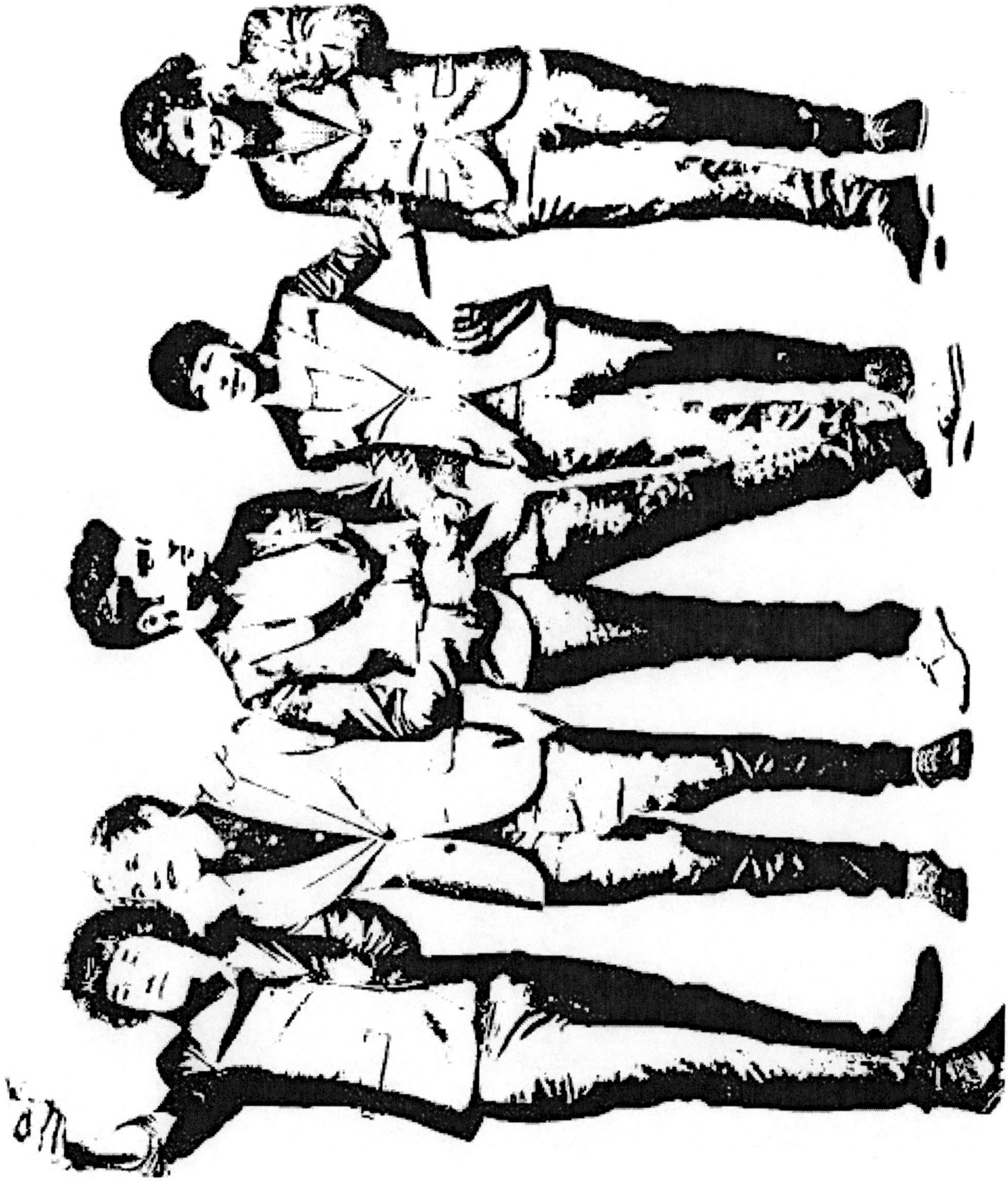

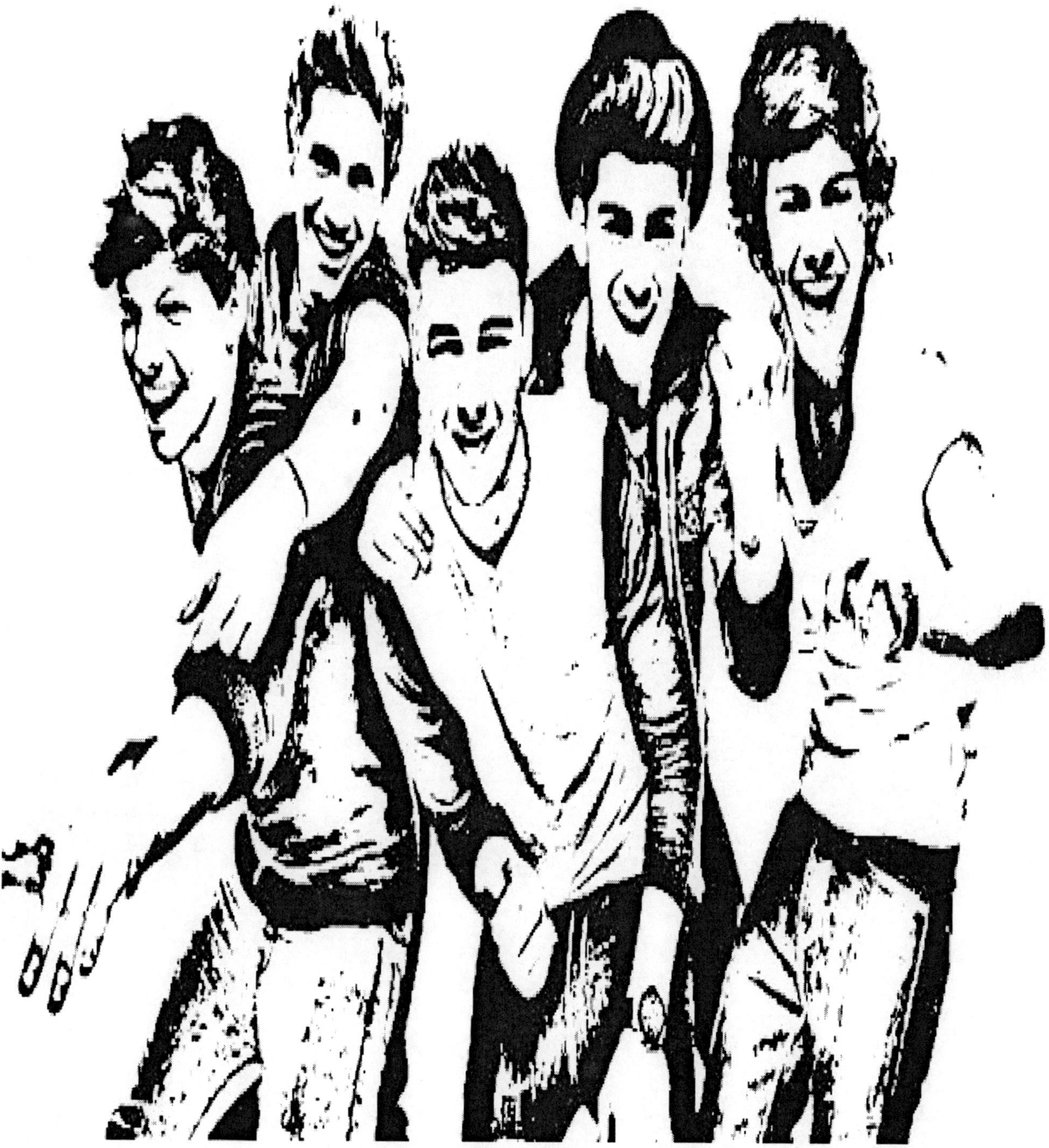

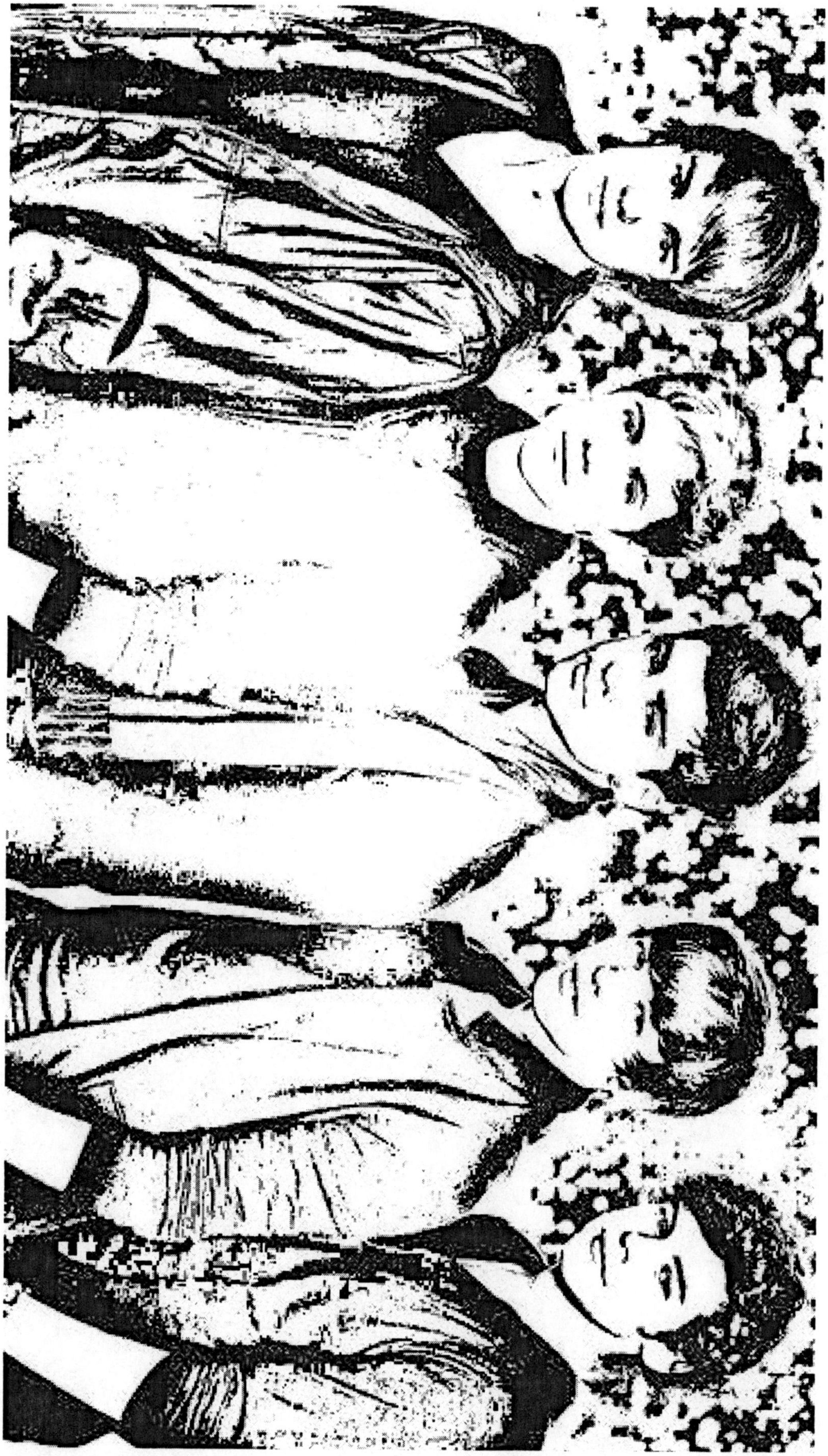

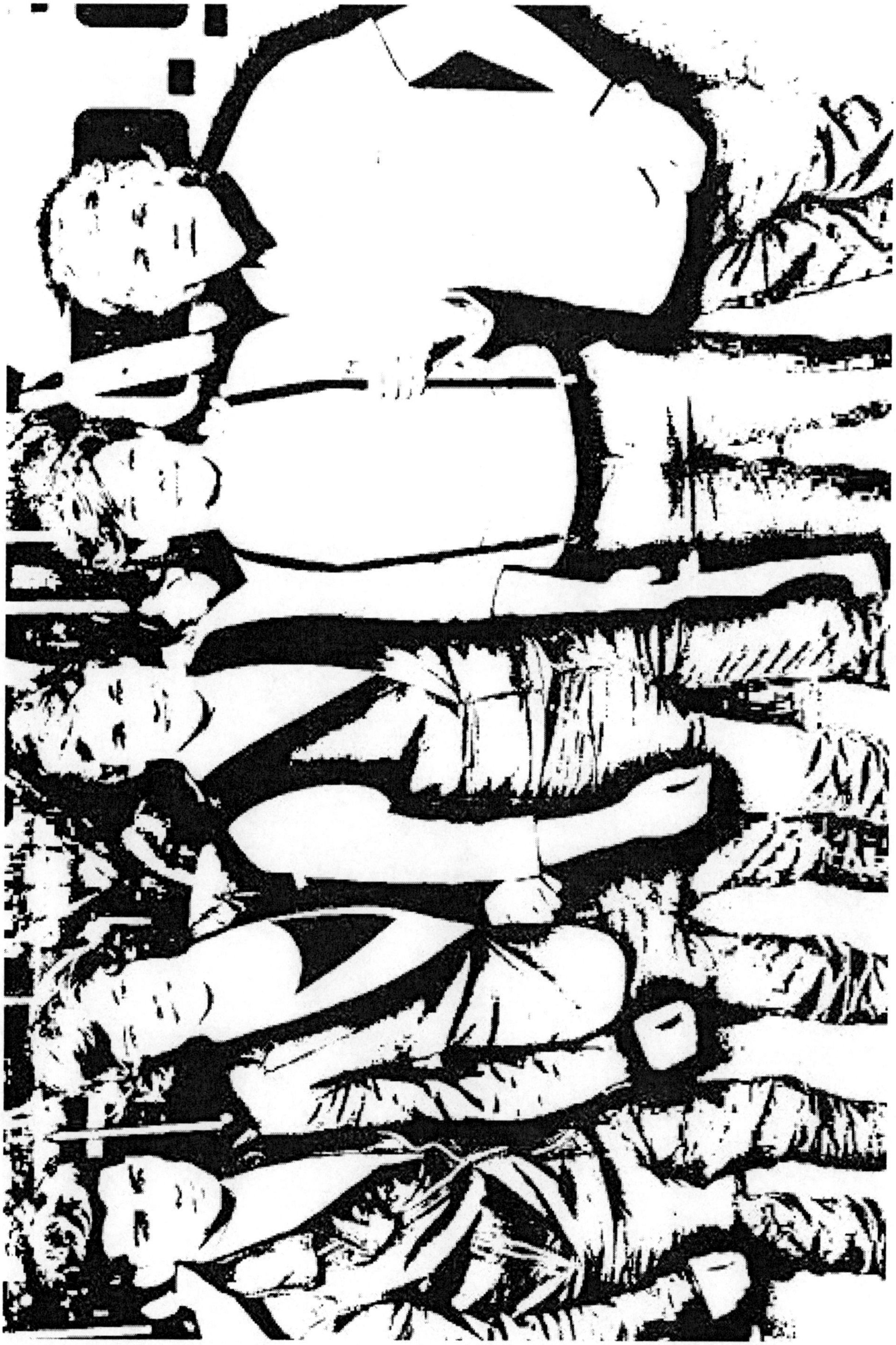

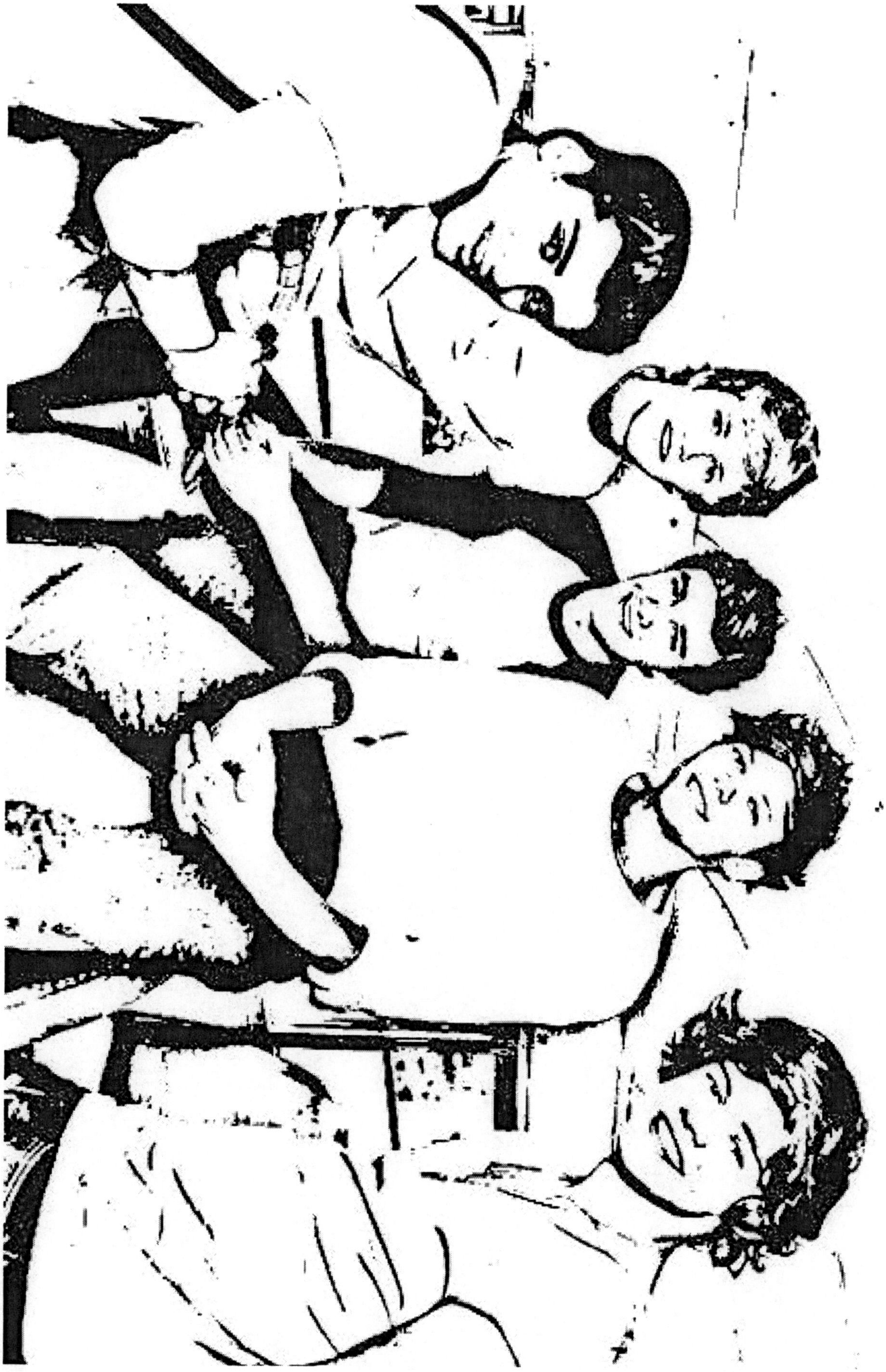

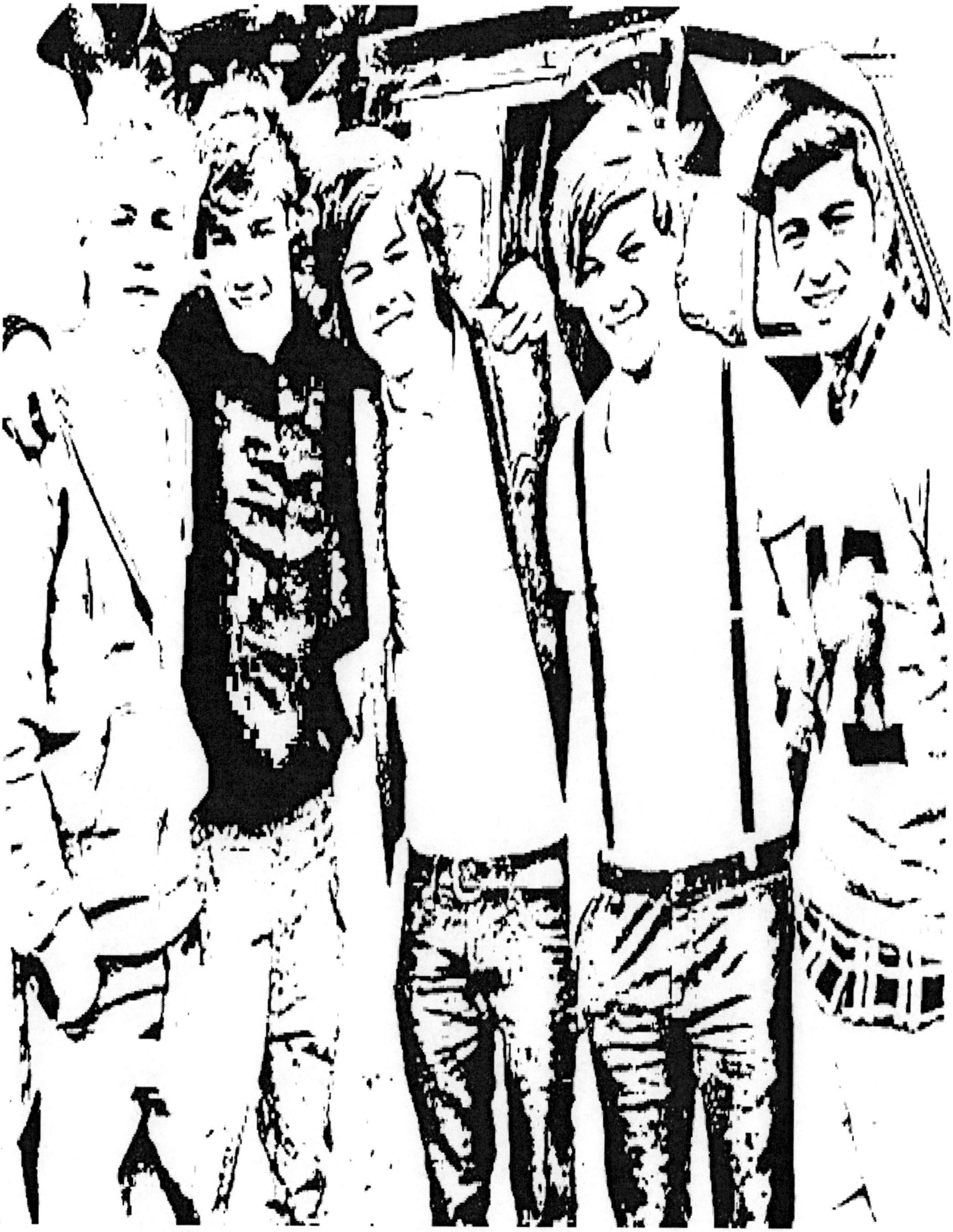

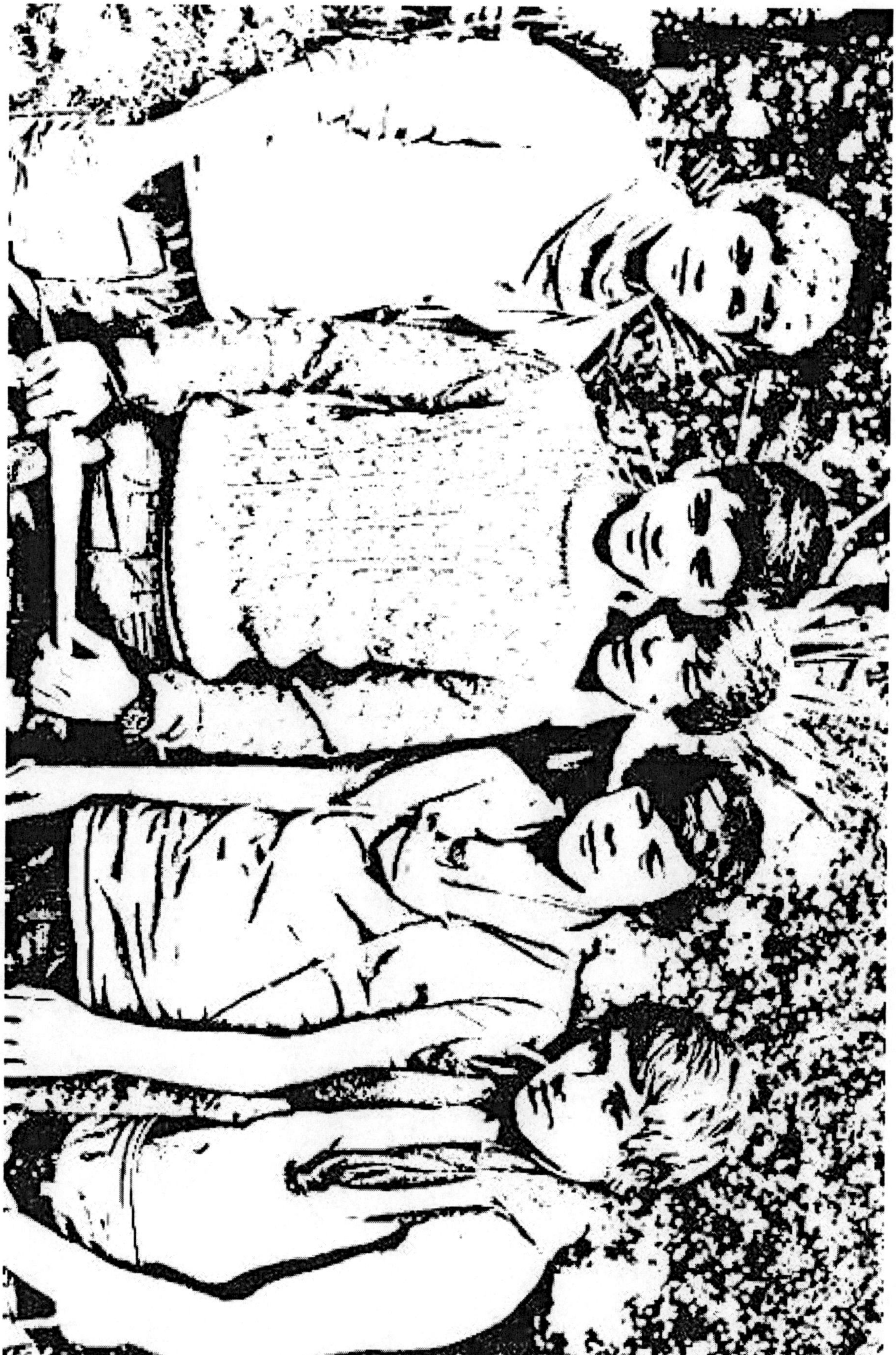

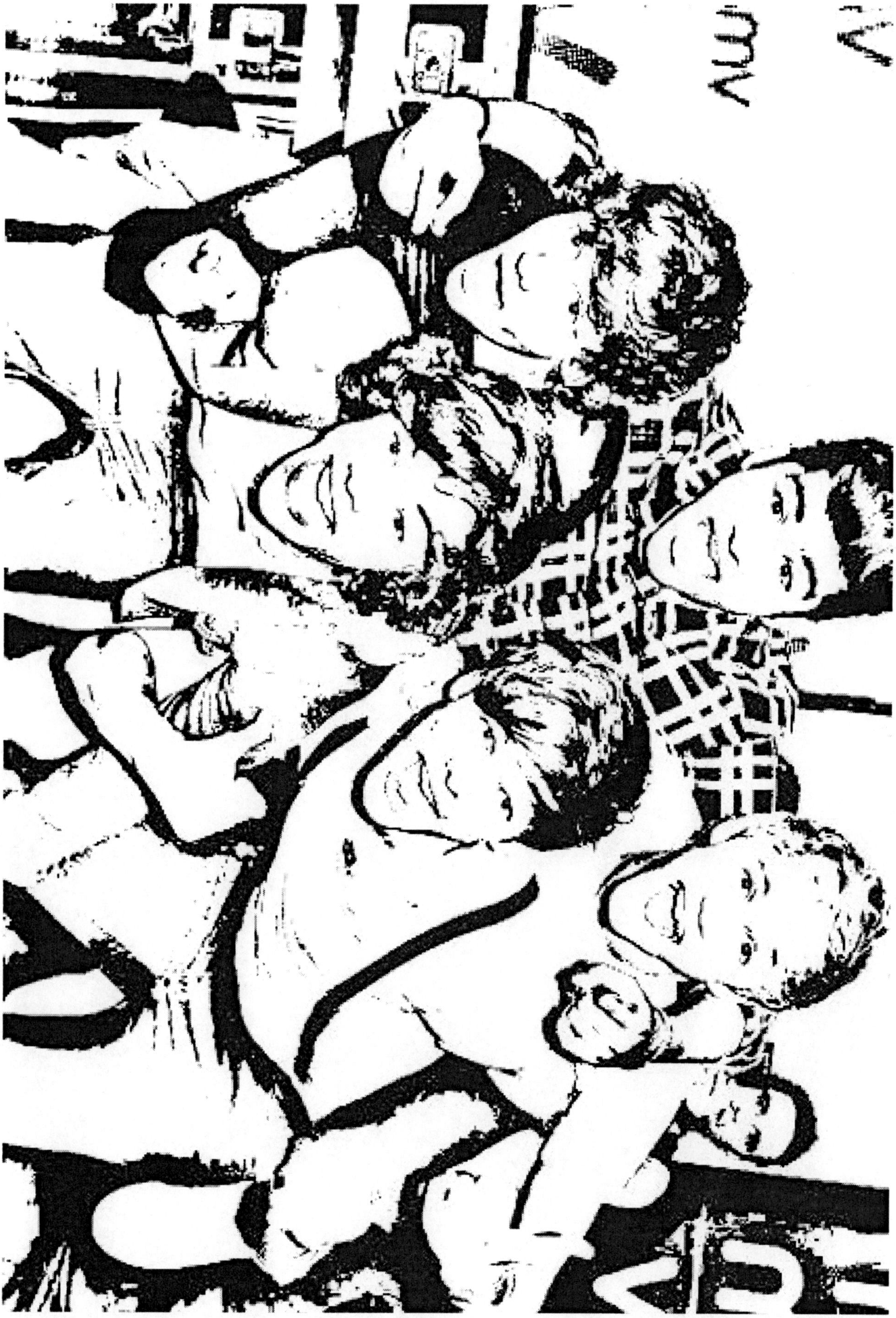

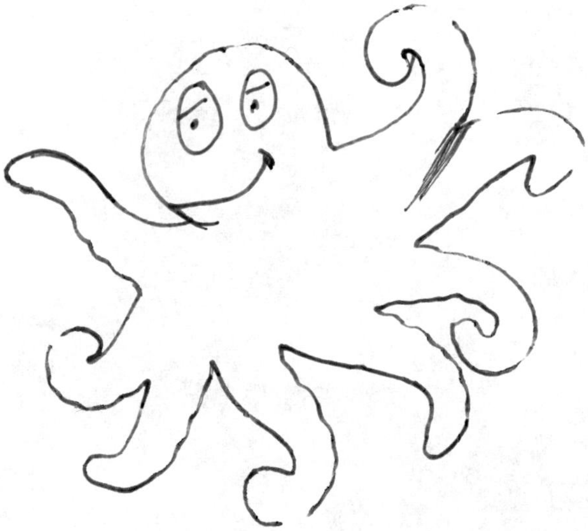

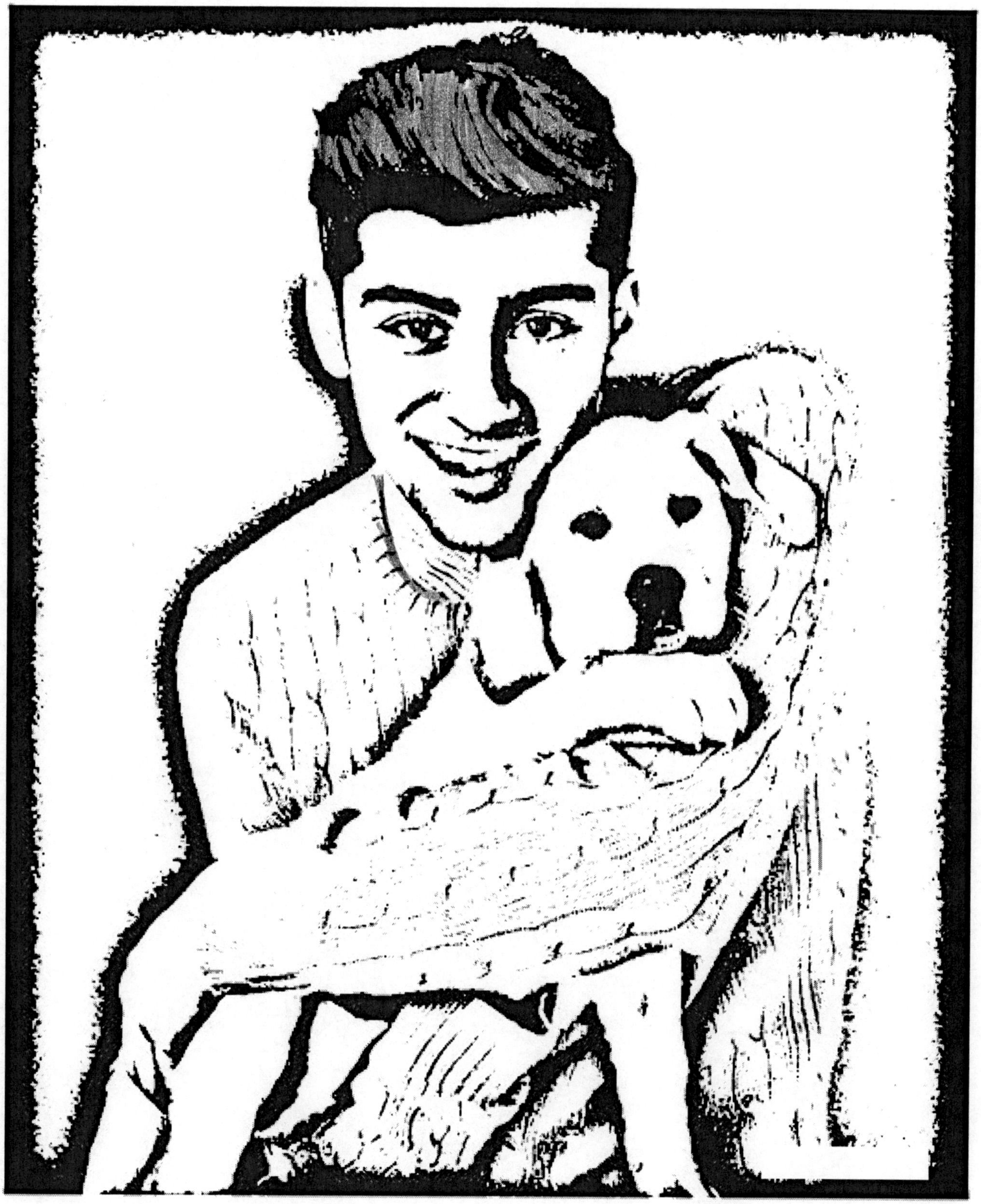

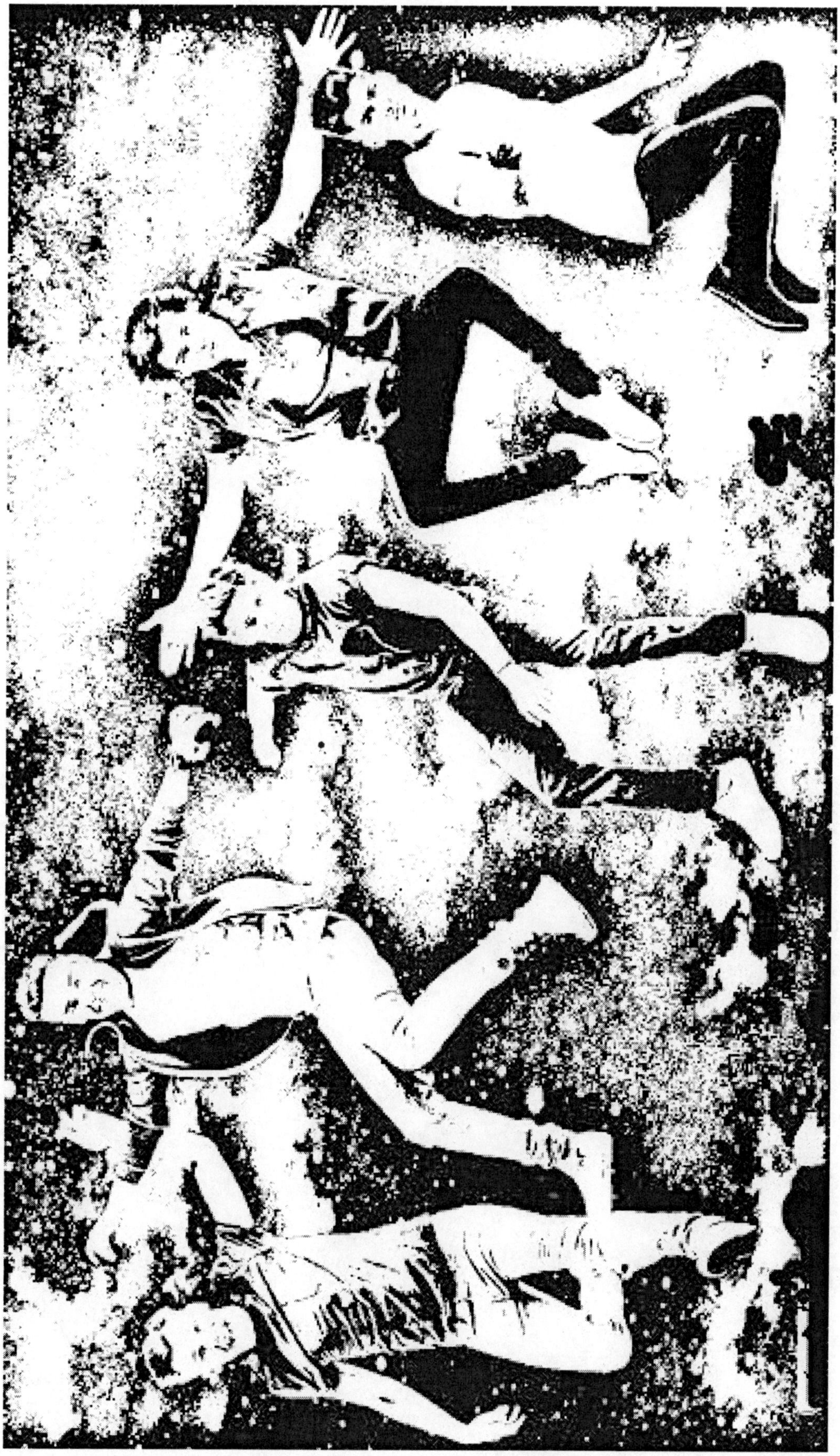

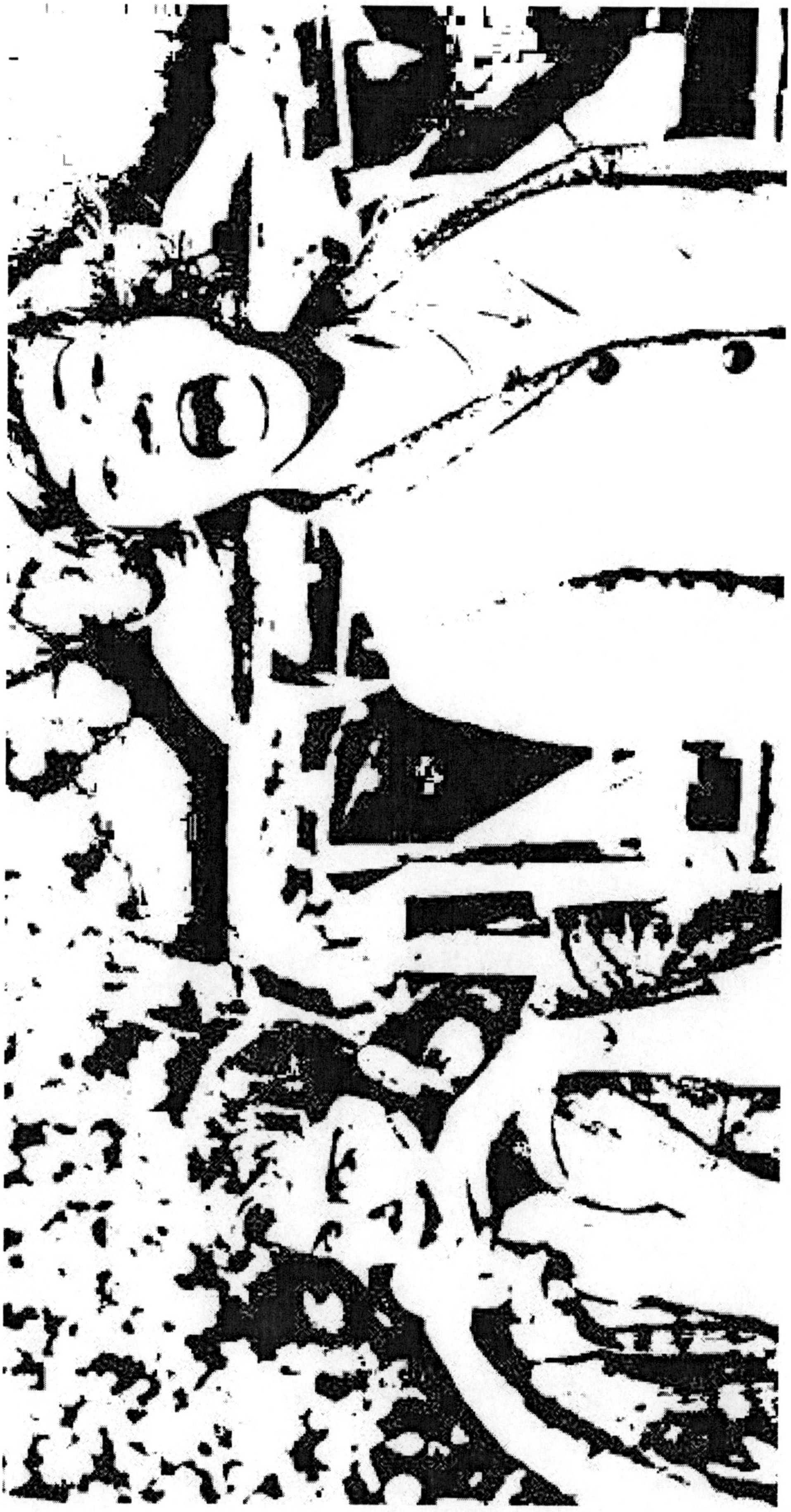

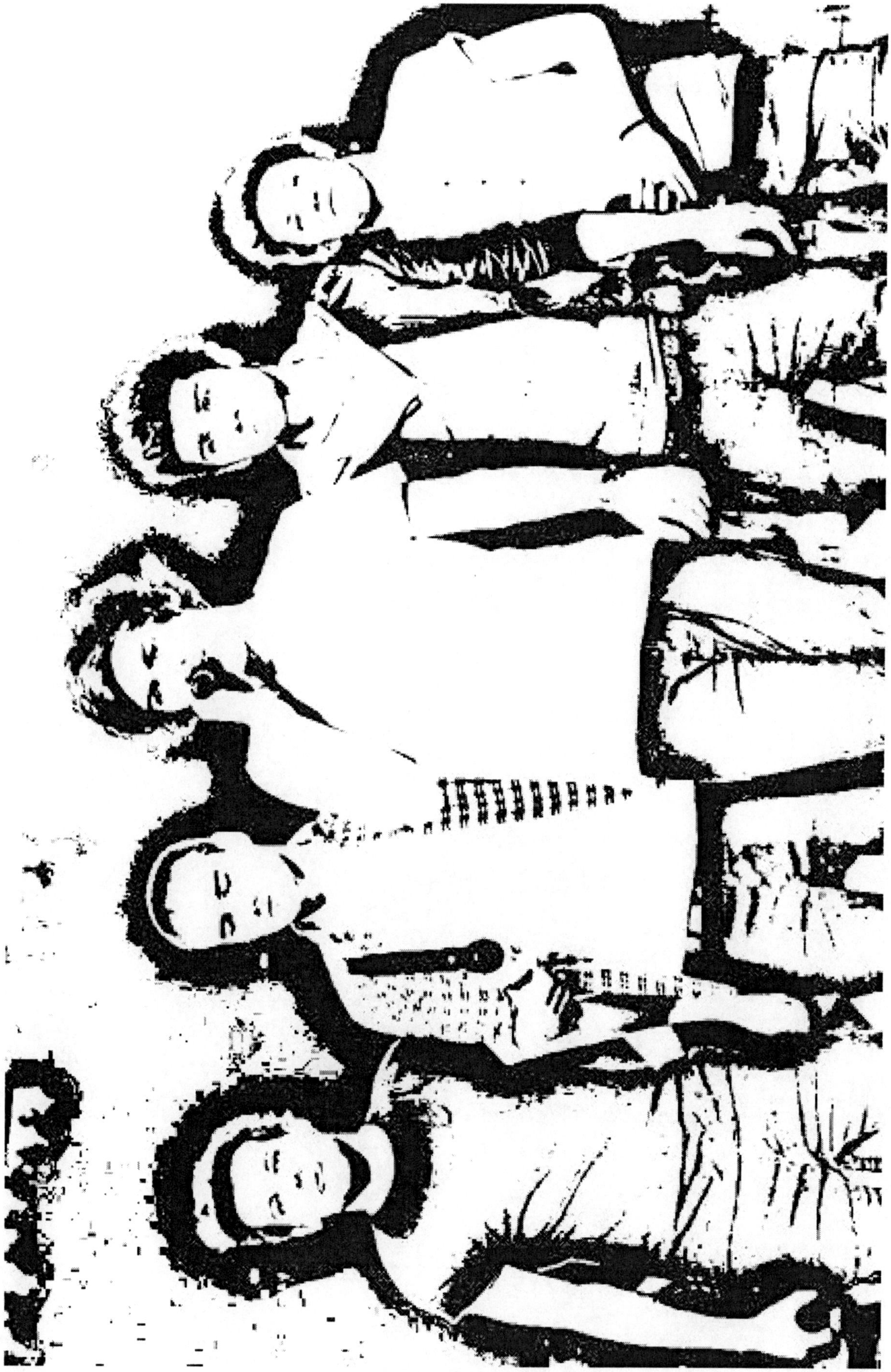

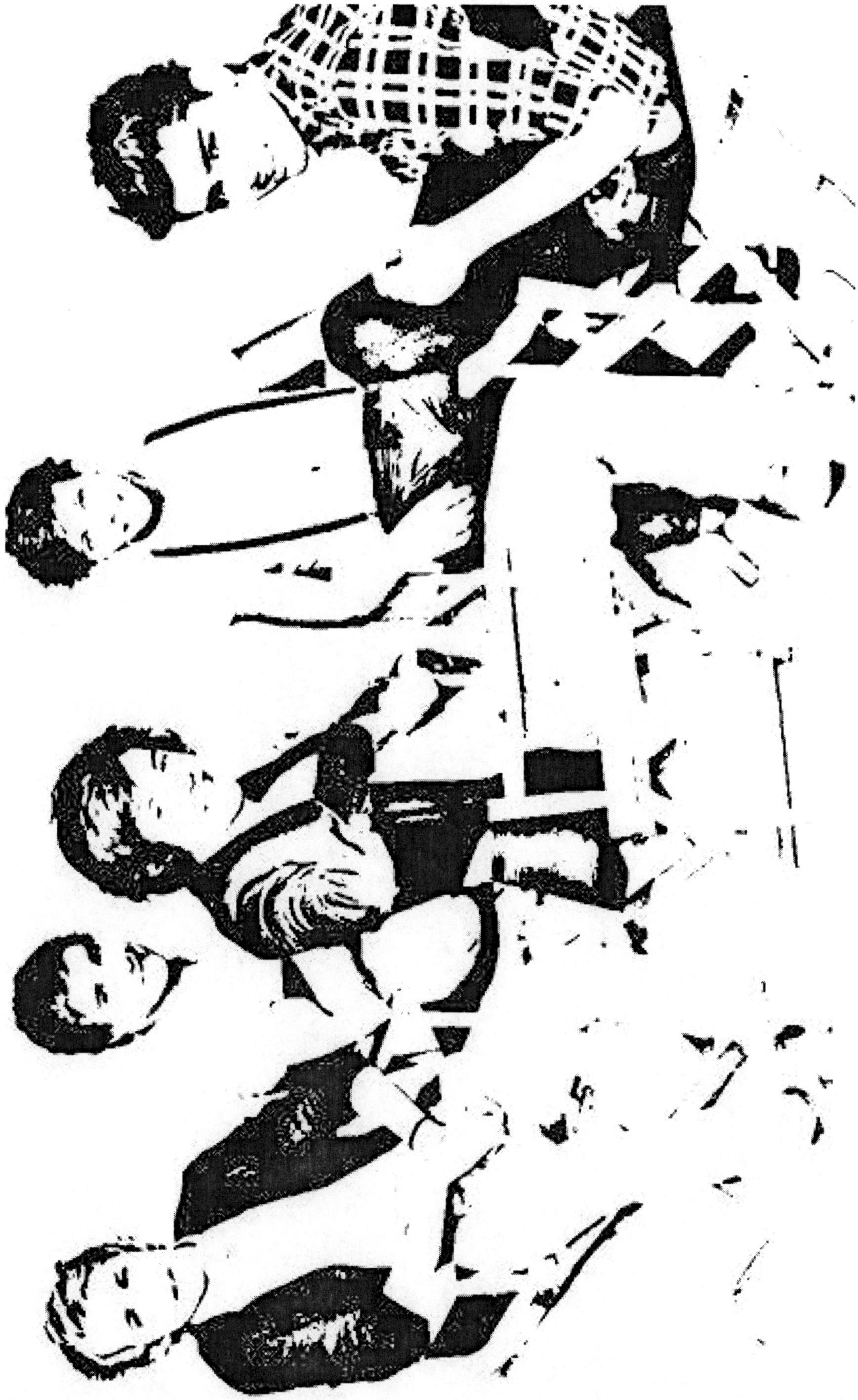

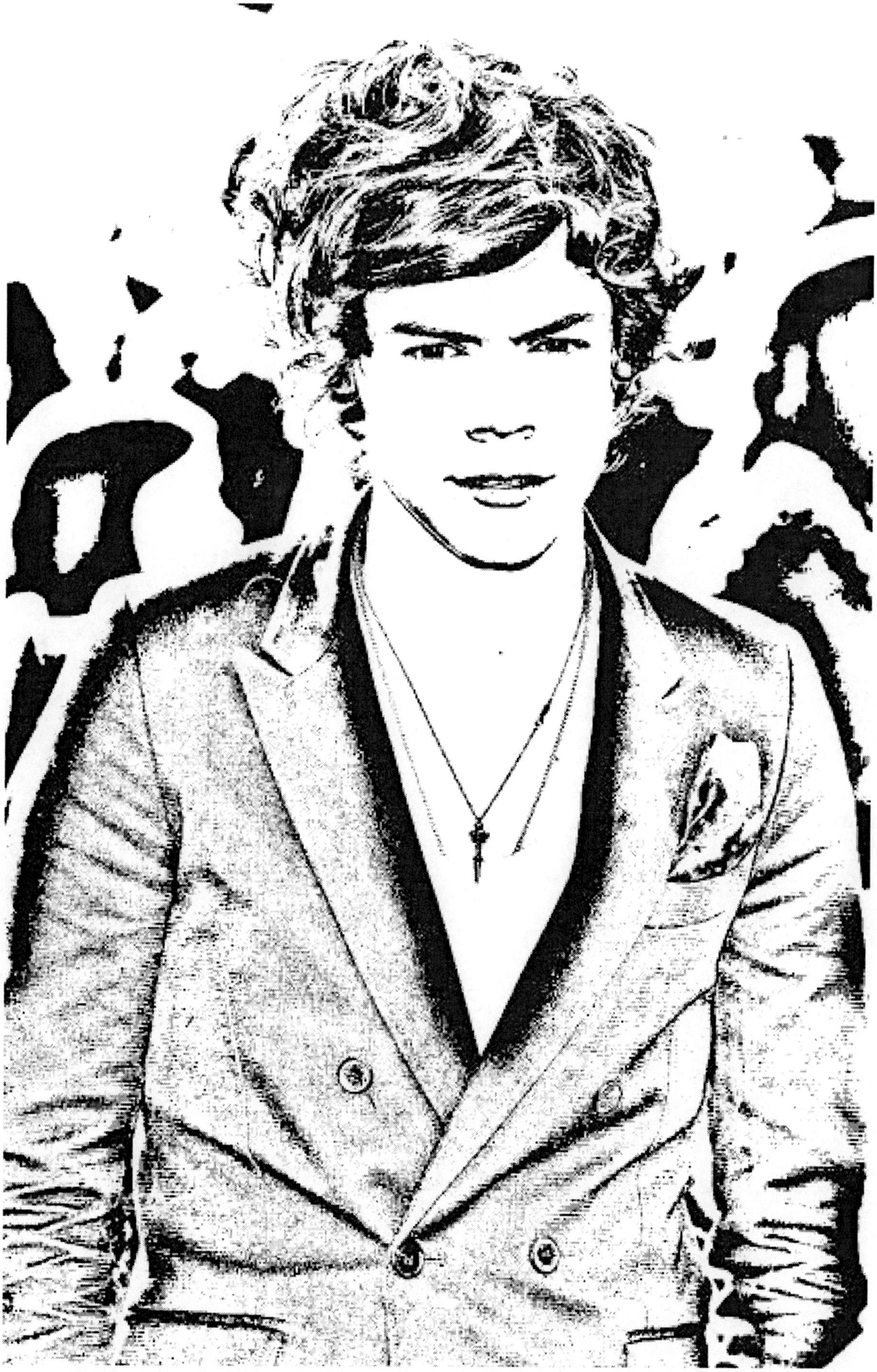

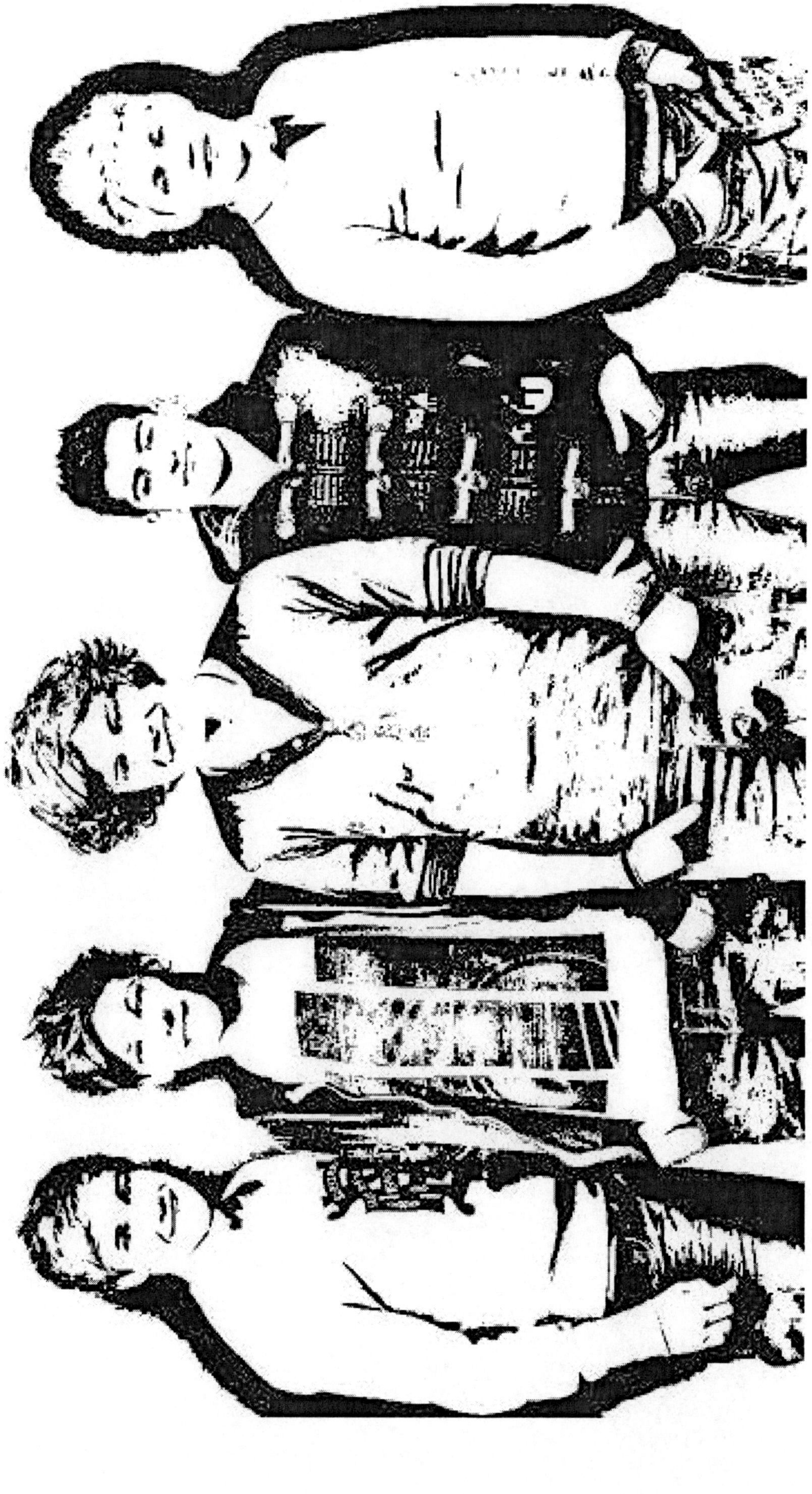

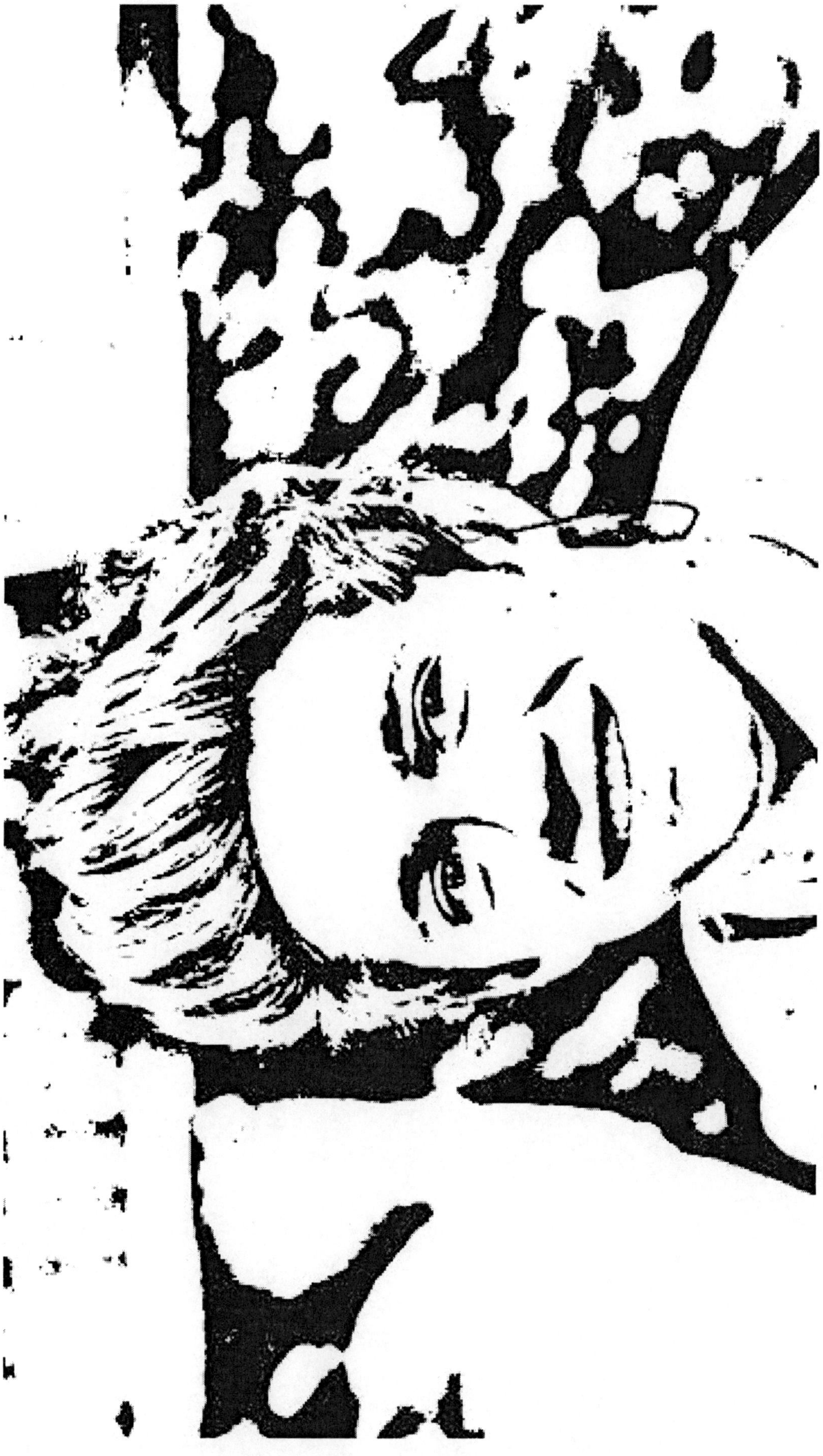

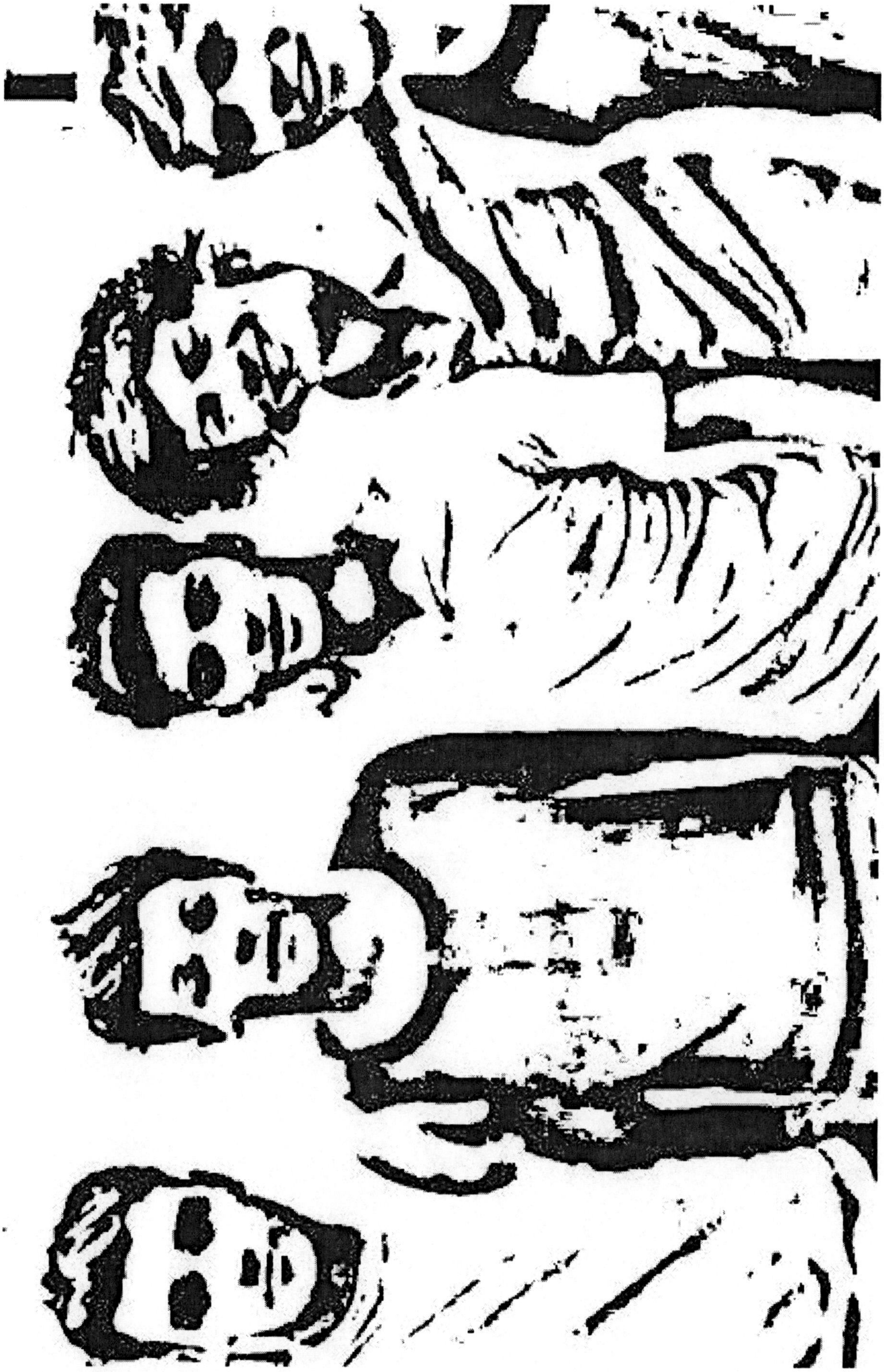

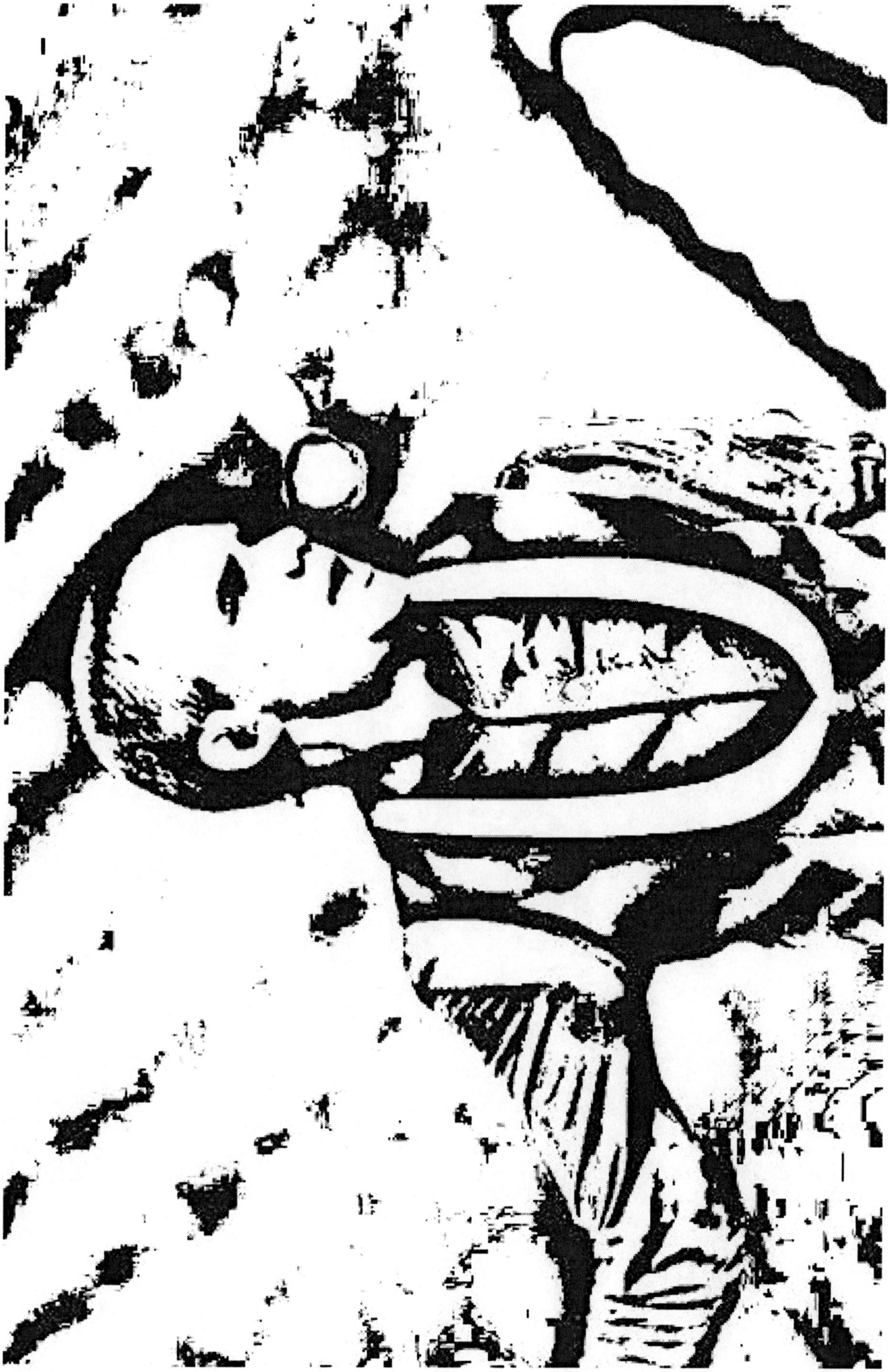

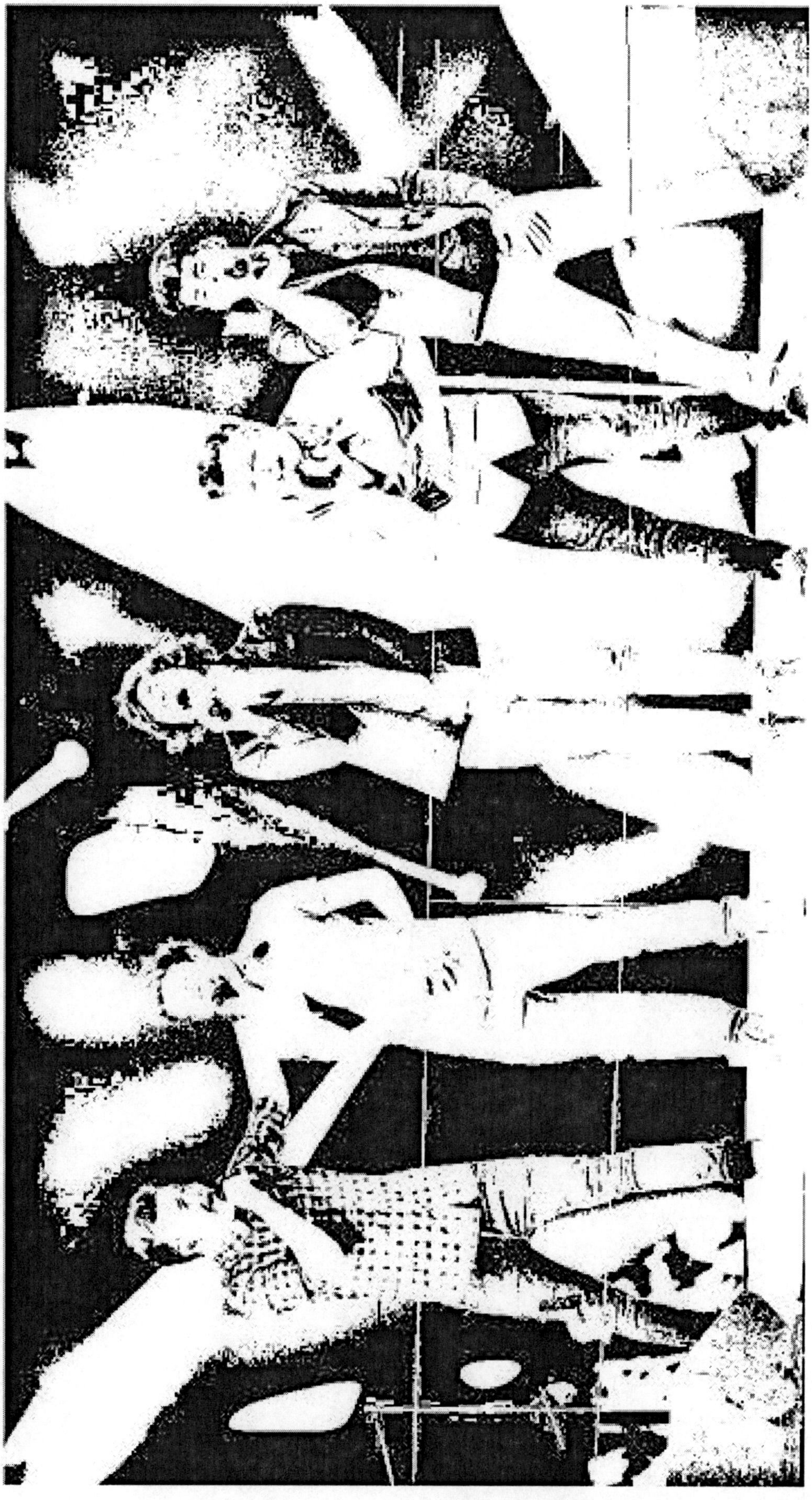

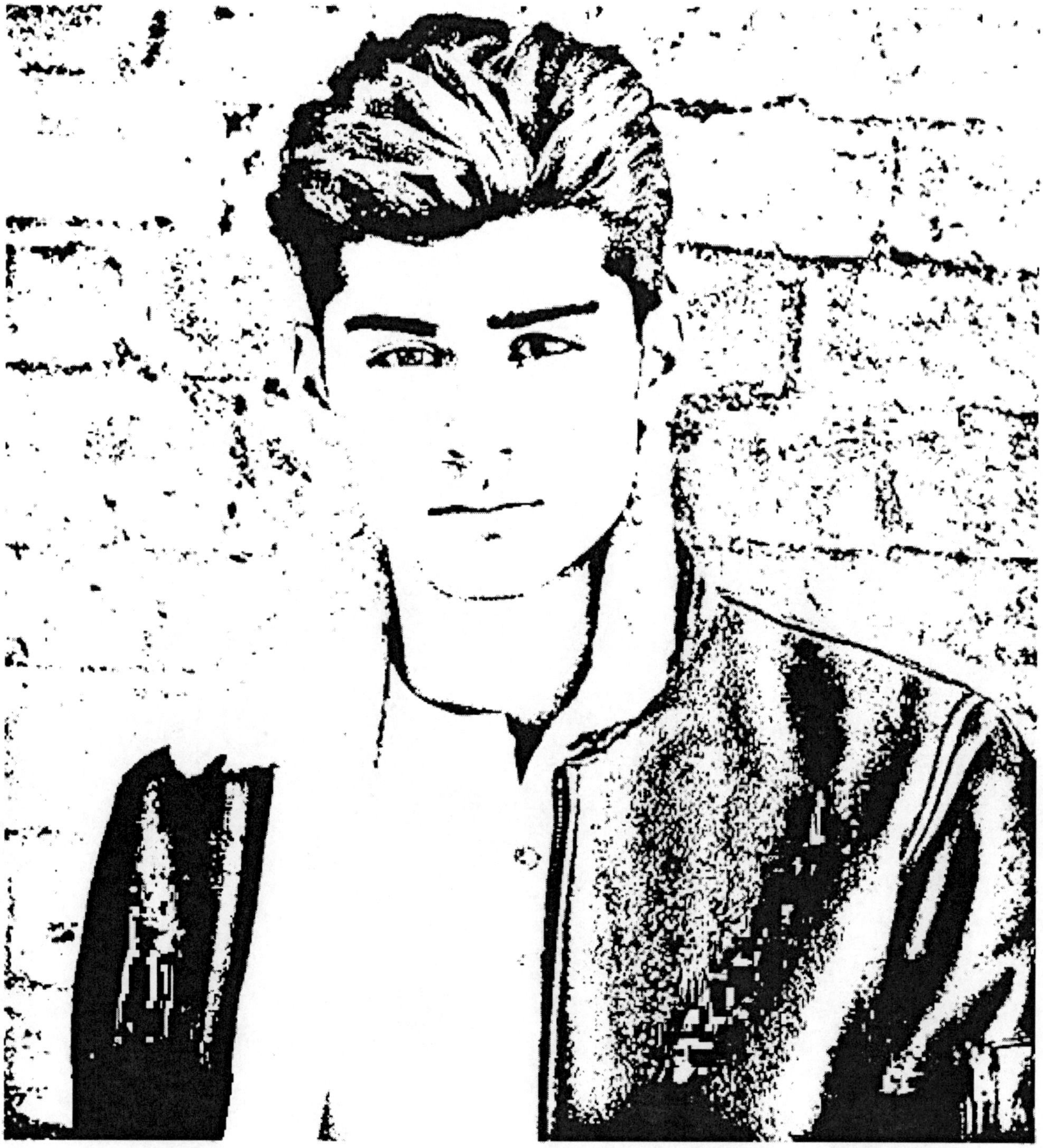

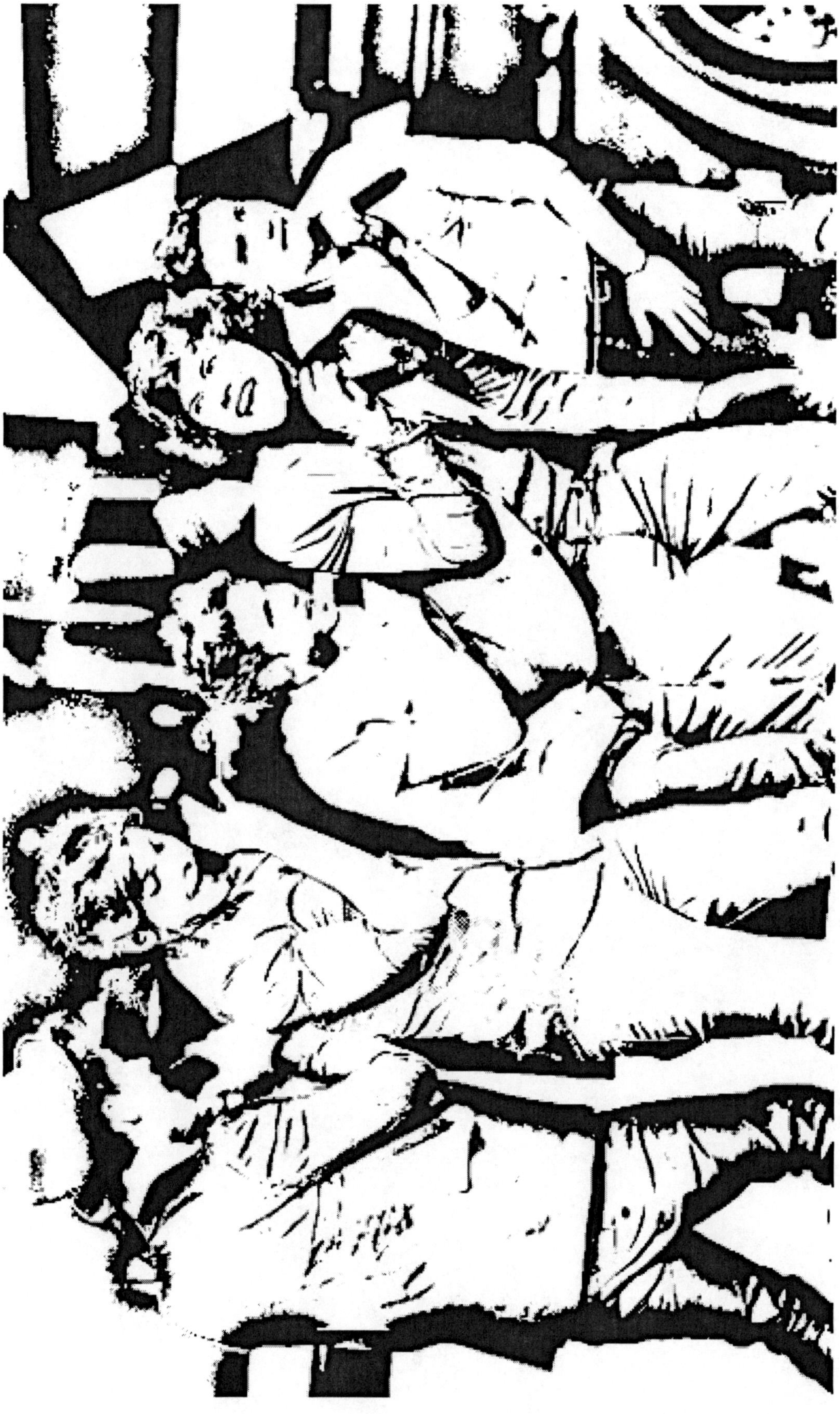